A TEACHER IN EAST AFRICA

Stories from the
Teachers for East Africa Experience

Learning from the
First Free Students in the 1960s

MOSES L. HOWARD

Jugum Press

ISBN: 978-1-939423-81-8

Published by Jugum Press
505 Broadway East #237
Seattle, Washington

Find ebook editions at www.jugumpress.com
Contact: JugumPress@outlook.com

This book is dedicated to my wife,
Immaculate Musanabera Howard,
whose favorite African proverb is:
"If you wish to move mountains
You must start by lifting stones."

Contents

These stories were originally written for the *Teaaki Wiki: stories and lessons learned from the Teachers for East Africa Experience of the 1960s.*

You can read other former teachers' stories at: http://bit.ly/2emMdzL

A TEACHER
IN EAST AFRICA

No Entry Permit

I first came to Entebbe, Uganda as a Fulbright scholar and teacher in 1961 on a BOAC flight from London. My trip had taken me, an African American lecturer at a community college in Mississippi, to the Foreign Service School in Georgetown University, then to the Foreign Service office in London, and soon, I hoped, to Ntare School in Mbarara, Uganda.

On the flight, I could identify the nationalities of many of the passengers: British, African, Belgians, Germans, and French. I think I was the only American among them, and certainly the only African American, or a so-called American Negro. So imagine everyone's shock when I was detained at the port of entry. The airport officials could not stamp my entry visa. The appropriate offices had issued me all the necessary traveling documents except one. I had a visa but no entry permit. I was detained for four hours while an officer wired London for further instructions regarding my permission to enter Africa.

After four hours, I was summoned and told I was to be given a temporary entry permit and had to swear to an affidavit that I was, indeed, who I said I was. They photographed me numerous times in specific positions and attached three photos to the affidavit, making a copy which they said I had to carry at all times. They also confiscated my passport and said they would contact me within ten days at the place I was posted.

It was in those circumstances that I contemplated that ages ago my ancestors had been kidnapped, taken forcibly from Africa, and now, when their son returned, others could enter without problems while he had to have a special permit to do so.

I went to my post, and six weeks later my passport arrived at the nearest post office. I signed my name, and then was finger printed and given the passport. I checked the pages and found that the British Consulate and the American Embassy had stamped it. I was finally in Africa legally. A descendent of slaves, a son of Africa, had returned three hundred years later and had been given a permit to enter.

Almost a Contender

Just six months before Uganda's independence in 1961, I was posted to Ntare School in Mbarara, Uganda. Ntare students, eager performers in class and just as quick in describing the geographical beauty of their country, persuaded me to visit with them in Kigezi. In a Volkswagen, we set out for Kabale and Kigezi's volcanic mountains.

The country was in a festive celebratory mood. Roadways and towns overflowed with jubilant people dressed in colorful shirts, skirts, and dresses. Many waved signs and shouted "UPC" (for Uganda People's Congress) and "DP" (for Democratic Party). The names "Obote" and "Kiwanuka" rang out from the roadside as the car coasted by. That past week at school, students jokingly accused me of looking exactly like Kiwanuka, the DP candidate for President of Uganda. Shouting people invaded the roadway, causing my car to weave among them. "They think you are Kiwanuka," the students said. Then they questioned my driving ability. They said I needed a driver. "You look like Kiwanuka and he has a driver." From the roadside, people shouted his name at me.

A cleared market place was decorated with standing banana trees in a circle. Women in colorful dresses danced up and down. blocking our way. More chanting: "Kiwanuka! Kiwanuka!" Surrounding our car, pressing close, they demanded I get out and make a speech.

"This is not Kiwanuka. We arrived ahead of him," my students explained over protest. They said I was an African-American teacher and Kiwanuka was on his way. The people allowed us back onto the Mbarara road when they discovered I could not speak Ruchiga or Runyankore.

Driving to Mbarara, I said to the students, "Hey, I could have been president of your country."

In a sobering tone of regret, a student announced the only requirement I didn't meet: "Sir, you don't know the language."

ON THE BRINK

"The arrival of the Americans is an important event:
its impact on the culture of the hill was really huge."

Ngugi wa Thiong'o,
as quoted by Mawuena Logan in
"Postcoloniality and Resistance in Earl Lovelace's
The Wine of Astonishment and *The Dragon Can't Dance*."
http://bit.ly/22x7kGc

We arrived in East Africa when the countries were on the brink of reaching independence. We taught teachers who witnessed this change as youth and would grow up to teach the history of that time, and yet we have focused little on that aspect when writing in retrospect about our experiences. We arrived at a time when Jomo Kenyatta, "the Burning Spear," was participating in governing the newly liberated Kenya, and when the great African Mwalimu Julius Nyerere was stressing *Uhuru na Kazi*. We were there when the first experiment in East African unity sprouted and grew. These countries threw off their former status as colonies and protectorates and became recognized members of the British Commonwealth.

Beyond that, we were there at a time of coups, bush wars, and revolutions. We were there at that great historical moment when the great labor organizer Tom Mboya helped to send thousands of African scholars to America for study, and he might have been instrumental in sending our future president's father to America. We were there in Africa; we saw it, we were a part of it, but we are reluctant to write about it. Are we afraid we will not be politically correct globally in our thinking? Afraid we might make a mistake?

It is true we might make mistakes, but this: having lived it, we know more about it than others.

> For more insights about the issues of East African students whose educational advancement hinged on the ability to bridge cultural gaps and make judgments and comparisons, and in some instances, to choose between values in their culture and an alien one, see also:
>
> Hamburger, Henry, "Culture Gap in Kakamega," *Technology Review*, June 1965. http://cs.gmu.edu/~henryh/culture-gap/

EMPAKOS

When I first came to Uganda and was a divorced young lecturer at Ntare School, I used to hang out and drink tea with a young nurse who worked at Mbarara Hospital. Her name was Lisa Kawumara.

On our first cup of tea she asked me my name, and I told her my name was Moses. She reflected for a moment, sipping her tea, then puffing her face and pointing at me with her small pert nose, she said, "*Yawe! Musa!* No. You're a Moses, but I am calling you Akiiki." And as we sat, she kept looking at me and referring to me when she had a question about America or my students at Ntare. She would say, "And so, Akiiki, what forms are you teaching?" And I would tell her I was teaching the fifth and sixth forms. And so after that, she left notes at my house addressed to Akiiki or she told other nurses that Akiiki was sure to stop by and to give me a message that she had left for me. Once she told me to call her Aboowli.

When I asked her about these names, she said they were *empako*. Upon further questioning, she said, "They are like nicknames or pet names, you know, terms of endearment." I wanted to know why she had selected these, and she said there were more, but these fit us. I wanted to know why, and when I would not relent, she told me there were many such names and they differed in other tribes, but she would just give me a few. As far as I can remember these are the names and the meanings she gave to me:

Abooli means a cat or quiet person.
Atwooki considered a naughty person.
Abooki means like a horn or fat or quiet.
Apuuli means a baby boy or little nice dog.
Abbala means keeper of cattle.
Acaali means dog.
Araali means thunder or lightning.
Amooti, *Akiiki*, and *Okali* are names given to very
special people.

Lisa Kawumara-Aboowli told me there were twelve or more *empakos*. She did not know the meanings of all of them, because some were names of evil spirits and should never be pronounced.

O LEVELS AND ME

In our staff room at Ntare High School, following examinations, British teaching masters pulled long, dissatisfied faces. The O-level English examination results never reached a desired level. It never failed, no matter how many passes students achieved in other subjects or even how well scores rose in Language, the students never reached the sought-after level of their counterparts in England. Therefore, the teachers of English and writing thought scores were abysmal in English and writing. In African schools, according to their voiced complaints, scores had always fallen low in language usage and writing.

As usual, a lot of discussion was generated about how to raise these scores for the next exams, a year away. One morning, the conversation centered on how students had not understood the classic English text, *Tom Brown's Schooldays* by Thomas Hughes. Members of staff read aloud, with picky laughs of derision, how students had responded to the behavior of Tom and the school bully Flashman. The students' written responses criticized Tom and Flashman, saying they would not be tolerated in an African school. The Prefect would "shut them down." The students did not take into consideration cultural differences or class background, or elements they misunderstood in the language nuance of the English author.

Although teachers had provided students with cultural information about English public schools and detailed the physical surroundings of those schools, the students evidenced no clear understanding of that information or how to use it accurately in critical written commentary about that classic novel. They clearly were not English boys who had imbibed this knowledge in rowhouse front parlors or by breathing English air. They were not English boys who had listened daily, from birth, to the conversations of parents and neighbors across backyard fences. They had not read English prose in unison with other British boys in schools from primary levels upward.

Still, the masters, for the most part, were unsympathetic. They did not take into consideration what was before them: boys who came from villages where there were not centuries of knowledge about the evolution of English literature, boys who had scant knowledge of the history of those people or of their language. In front of them were African boys from villages who had never set foot on English soil. They had rarely heard the language spoken accurately and had never listened to their parents and neighbors speak English. "They nor their parents," one master noted, "are allowed at our clubs, where they'd see our crude attempts at rugby. And who among us even have witnessed, out here, anyone bowl a perfect score at cricket?"

I listened to all of this with interest until old Robson, one of the elder lecturers, stated the whole thing more clearly. "These chaps are rather good, actually. I doubt that any of us, in their stead, could do better."

"How do you say that?" Other masters quickly challenged him.

"These blokes are actually expected to do the impossible," he went on. "They are born in African villages where only Bantu languages are spoken, not written. They live there, listening to uneducated vernacular all their formative lives, and then, they are asked to become English boys by the time they are thirteen, speaking and writing polished English as if they were in a Rugby school, with the background of a Tom Brown and a Flashman."

"Hear, hear! We know that. It's been said often enough before, but what's the answer, Robby?" they queried him.

"It's plain enough what's needed. But how to supply it is a major drawback."

"Well, well, a solution to our annual worries is imminent. Tell us, Robby, tell us what's needed."

By now, Robson was laughing that everyone was turning his attempt at levity into a referendum on his ability to solve the insolvable problems of low O-level English scores. "I don't think it bloody fair for you chaps to mark me as the Oracle at Delphi because I point to what is commonly known by all of us."

"Just tell it. What is the creaking bloody answer? I warrant you we all stand to be indebted to you for it."

"Well, now I need to shorten this." He looked all around at them. "What is needed is an examination set on a book written about them and their environment. I am sure that would go a long way toward improving English and writing scores."

"The catch is there is no such book in existence."

"Then someone should write one."

"Who, by all means?" Eyes darted around the staff room. "Who knows the intimate relations of the lives of these chaps? You would have to sleep in their huts, eat cassava, *ntulas*, cabbages, their plantain and groundnut soup. You'd have to see them born, see them married, go to funerals. None of us have done this."

Someone else looking around seized on a lecturer who to this point had been uninvolved. "The nearest description to that is Bottram." All eyes fell on the geography master, who taught bare-chested in class, wore colored togas, and behaved much as if he was Lawrence of Arabia in town and on safari.

Bottram declined, saying with emphasis, "I write factual geography books. I have long been of the opinion that exams should be written on scholarly investigations and information of nonfiction rather than on fabricated tracts. What I write can be shown, measured, and verified. Half of *Tom Brown's Schooldays* is sentimental haberdashery. It's propaganda, preachments on manners and morals, written to influence rather than to educate and inform."

While the whole staff looked at him, smiling, he added, "That's your field, fiction," he pointed an open geography book at Robson and waved it at the other English masters. "That's your department. If Jim Hilton were here, you could possibly get him to write a *Goodbye, Mr. Mulumu* instead of *Goodbye, Mr. Chips*, and you would have your local novel. But, frankly, it will have to be someone closer, someone among them someone who lives in an African village.

"How about Ngugi's *Weep Not, Child?*"

"I am afraid not. It's too cerebral and psychological for the purpose. It has to be simple, everyday, down to earth," Old Robson put in. He was a respected old don from Oxford who had himself been prepped at Eton and knew English schools.

Then, Robin Dawes, who was always kidding me about how I spent every moment in the village, even spending nights with friends and student families there, now spoke up. "Moses should be the one for that task. He knows the village better than any of us."

"Can't you deliver us from this dilemma, Moses?" they shouted with laughter.

I thought it was a great joke and said so, since I taught chemistry and biology. The other English masters thought so, too.

"But that would be even worse." They pursued that old American joke. "He's an American, and you know they don't speak English over there, not even as well as any of the other colonies." There was quiet in the staff room, with all of the English masters looking at me and the three other American teachers to see if we regarded the comment an insult. After a pause, we all laughed and the subject was dropped.

While the staff room conversation had taken an unusual turn, it had been an ordinary day. I went back to preparing chemistry lessons and going to sports in the evening with the boys. I was helping them learn basketball, which had been recently introduced to Uganda, and they tolerated me in their soccer games. Every free moment, as was my habit, I escaped to a nearby village called Ruti, another name for trees. A family had adopted me on my first visit. They had made me welcome, and I joined the family of four boys and five girls, two of whom were already primary schoolteachers. I worked on their farm, cutting pineapples, gathering papaya, digging drainage ditches in the banana plantations, and milking goats.

Time with the family was always enjoyable. However, the father, a Gombola chief, was experiencing a problem with his son at secondary school who was having difficulty deciding between being a British boy or an African one. He had adopted the habits of his British masters, copying their speech and trying to be a dandy at home in the village, neglecting to care for the goats or to pick coffee berries. It was a problem similar to one experienced by my brother back in America with his teenaged son who neglected his studies, trying for a career in music instead of keeping up his grades.

Back in the staff room at school, they kept up their ribbing, not letting go threads of the conversation about my writing a book, suitable for evaluating African students in English. "Moses," they would say, "how is the African school-days book progressing?" They often asked that question instead of greeting me or engaging in an exchange about the chemistry and biology classes I was teaching. I knew I was not a writer with skills approaching those of Thomas Hughes, and I knew I didn't know enough about Africa to write such a book, even if I had possessed the skills. But they kept asking as if they intended to goad me into doing it. I had told myself that I couldn't do it, but I was offended by their constant inference that I could.

So one evening, instead of going to Ruti, I began a narrative about the place. I wrote about what I knew. I based my story on what was happening there, knowing I could never reach a level anywhere near the almost perfect scenes and themes in *Tom Brown's School Days*. Nevertheless, I went on.

Over the holidays, I wrote every chance I got, and I produced a text of more than a hundred pages and thirty thousand words. It was a story about a boy in an African village who wanted to be British. He mimicked his school masters and lost his father's confidence and his father's goats to marauding dingoes, to wild dogs roaming the countryside. The boy feared the vicious dogs and thus feared becoming a man. I called the story *Dogs of Fear*. In Ruti, the people called me Musa (for Moses), and because I was always on the go, they called me Nagenda, which means going. So I put a fly leaf on my book, entitling it *Dogs of Fear* by Musa Nagenda. I dumped the manuscript on Old Robson's desk when he was at prep one evening.

Two days later, with his usual good humor, he said, "It doesn't measure up, old chap. It's not anywhere near Tom Hughes's *Tom Brown*, but it has a quest." It was two days before school holidays, and so nothing else was said until we came back six weeks later. During that time, I had come down with a swollen toe, so painful I couldn't walk to class. I called the headmaster and said I would be absent. That evening Denis Wills, one of the English master, came to see me and diagnosed my condition as gout. He brought me medicine from the apothecary and a list of foods to avoid. Among those forbidden were beef and liver, two of my favorites.

As Denis was leaving, he called me Musa Nagenda and said James Currey, an editor from Heinemann's educational books, had been looking for me the previous day. The chap had a manuscript that he wanted to publish, but no one seemed to know the author. The book was *Dogs of Fear*. Robson had been away, and no one else besides Denis knew that I was the author. Denis, in fact, was a writer himself. I had discussed writing with him a few times in the midst of writing the book. He knew I was the author, but didn't know if he should tell that to Currey. When Robson returned, he confessed to sending the manuscript to Heinemann without my knowledge.

The book was published in a new junior series by Heinemann, and Gene Ashby brought the first copies to me where I was living in the holidays with my Tutsi wife and two children on my *shamba* in Ankole. That book was followed by two more: *The Ostrich Chase* and *The Human Mandolin*. Heinemann showed these books at a book fair in Frankfurt, Germany, where an American publisher, Holt, Rinehart and Winston saw them and brought out American-published copies.

Perhaps needless to say, *Dogs of Fear* was never up to a standard where it could be set as a book for a national examination, but it was sold over the world, was translated into Norwegian, and garnered the author fan mail from young readers in Australia and New Zealand. It was used as practice books for local exams, and in America, it was selected for a section in a sixth-grade reader called *Bright and Beautiful*. That was in the 1970s.

The first two books are out of print now, but anyone still interested can Google them. They are in libraries and knocking around on Amazon.com.

DAVID BRUCE'S MICROSCOPE

In 1965, on loan to UNESCO at Uganda Technical College, I helped to train the country's first locally trained-onsite laboratory technicians. Until then, laboratory technicians were trained and examined in London by the City and Guilds of London and other United Kingdom examining bodies. These trainees studied locally and were examined locally.

We had well-equipped chemistry and biology laboratories with the exception of adequate microscopes. Raiding some high school labs, we found fifteen passable microscopes. Most had low magnification and unsatisfactory resolving power. It was a busy year with teacher and students collecting and testing the country's milk, blood, infective tissues, microbes, and fungi of every type. From classrooms, we went to the Fisheries Department and Viral Institute at Entebbe.

Most trainees passed, and UNESCO examiners were satisfied. The examiners, however, criticized our lack of good microscopes. But I went to our best one and called an examiner over to have a look. It was a magnificent black-and-gold instrument with a large barrel and clear lenses. I watched him focus and refocus it, running an appreciative hand up and down the barrel of it and calling to his fellow examiners that we had indeed made a discovery.

I wanted to look into the microscope to see what he had discovered, but it was the microscope itself to which he referred. On the barrel was printed *DK Bruce FRS*—that is, David K. Bruce, Fellow in the Royal Society. The examiner pronounced it to be the same microscope that David K. Bruce had used in South Africa in 1801 to prove that trypanosomes carried by the tsetse fly caused *nagana* in cows and horses. He used it again in Uganda in 1803 to prove that trypanosomes carried by tsetse flies, *glossina*, cause sleeping sickness in humans.

It was significant: our first trained-onsite technicians were using that same microscope.

About Positive and Negative

"Excuse me, sir, I'm asking."

"Yes, Sendagire, go on."

It was our ten-minute session at the end of a chemistry class at Ntare School in Mbarara, Uganda in 1961, a time set aside for students to ask questions on any part of the lesson they didn't understand.

"It's about positive and negative, sir."

"Yes, go on. What is it about positive and negative?"

"It is confusing, sir. You have taught us that in an electric circuit electrons flow from the negative to the positive. Isn't that right, sir?"

"Yes, that is correct."

"But, sir, if negative flows to the positive, it must be moving, acting, sir. We have been led to believe if something is moving and active it is positive. And now in chemistry, if it is acting, doing, why isn't it called positive?"

"Oh, I see, and you are absolutely right. A long time ago, researchers discovered that there were two opposite types of electric charges, and they could have been called just as you say one black the other white, but they were designated positive and negative. Had those scientists been as analytical as you are now, they would have been named as you suggest, but they agreed to call them as we are calling them now, and it would be too confusing to change them."

"You said *agreed.* Is that the way much knowledge is based, on agreements made long ago?"

"What do you mean?"

"I am thinking about electrons. We can't see them, sir, but *they* agreed long ago that electrons exist."

"But there is evidence that they exist. We can test that evidence."

"But, sir, I am thinking about math also, sir. There are rules about which we have no proof, but they are accepted. We use them consistently to solve problems, sir."

"Such as what?"

"I think one word is *axiom,* a self-evident truth. I can't think of the other."

But here another boy, Mugisha, stepped in to help. "We talked about postulates, which I think are like axioms... and theorem, which is an idea or belief, or method generally accepted as true, but it needs a proof."

They chorused: "We cannot. How can we, as students, accept that, sir?"

A spirited discussion followed. "Proof, where was the proof?"

This conversation occurred in a high school chemistry class in which one student was to become the president of Uganda. I am sure I learned as much in that class as did the students, and yet I have in front of me a book written by the president, entitled *Sowing the Mustard Seed*, in which he has inscribed the following:

30/12/2009
To: Mzee Moses Howard
Of the USA (formerly of Ntare 1961–62)
From: President Museveni of Uganda

"You were a great chemistry teacher.
You solved the problem of valence for me."

President Museveni's book is a history of Uganda during and soon after the coup of Idi Amin. It covers years following the coup.

It describes the country during the revolution in which the president and his fellow students fought a bush war, deposed Amin, and are now serving as rulers of their country.

EAST INDIA AND AFRICAN LIFE

In 1961 throughout towns in East Africa were many East Indians. Locally, they were called Asians. They had originated in India, but may have recently immigrated from other countries that had an affiliation with the British Commonwealth. They were Sikhs, Hindi, and Muslims who followed the Agha Khan or others of Indian subcontinent origin. Some young East Indians came to school with Africans, especially in the technical colleges and the teacher training colleges, and they talked about their customs and religious beliefs.

African names sound different: Mukasa, Sentongo, Kajubi, Nagenda. East Indian names were Patel, Surrender Panzer, Desai, Sumitri. Even the places from where they came sound different to an African: India, Calcutta, Bengal, Gujarat, Dharma, and different countries such as Fiji, Columbia, Peru. There were even a few from Canada.

The British colonial rulers brought in the Asians. Some of them had British citizenship. A few had maneuvered their way into African citizenship, but most of them were stateless. British colonialists allowed them in and gave them preference over Africans in competing for civil service jobs, especially if they qualified. For example, Mr. Sumitir Joshi was a business graduate, and Mr. Summitry Chandra had a master's degree in chemistry and was head of department at the teacher training college where I taught.

Many of the Asians had better education qualification than the Africans. They qualified for jobs in the civil service that allowed them to clerk in offices. They worked in car dealerships and ran shops in the towns. They also generally lived in those towns: for example, in Uganda, towns such as Kampala, Mbarara, Masaka, Mubendi, Jinja; in Kenya, Nairobi, Mombasa, Nyeri; in Tanzania, Moshi, Dar es Salaam. In 1961 only a relatively small number of Africans lived in the towns. Africans for the most part lived in villages or on small farms near the towns.

Africans trekked into towns in the early morning every day. They lined the roadways and streets coming to work in the houses of the British civil servants or in the shops of the Asians or in their own shops. In the evening, the streets and roadways were again crowded with Africans hurrying back to their homes in villages miles away. In the morning, they walked or rode bicycles loaded with bananas, corn, tomatoes, beans, peas, chickens, or pineapples. Some arrived driving goats or packing all kinds of goods from their farms to be sold in the towns during the day. Some might ride buses or taxis, but very many more walked, laden with all kinds of farm produce to sell in the towns.

In the mornings, bicycles were loaded with goods for sale, but in the evening, going back to farm villages, bicycles had passengers. They were used as taxis to transport people home. Africans worked in shops in the town or in the homes of Asians or British expatriates. They cooked food, shopped for groceries, and kept house for their employers. A few of them had substandard homes in an unlit part of the town. East Indian people, on the other hand, worked in government offices and administered the postal service, or worked for the public works or water departments on roads, streets, and the electric system. The Asians' houses were well constructed of cement blocks and finished inside with plaster.

There were schools near the town for British children. East Indians often had their own private schools, but they also attended

African and British schools. School masters above junior high school were taught mostly by British or Asian teachers. Africans could attend if they could afford the very high fees. Most British children were sent to boarding schools in Kenya or back to England, Ireland, or Scotland. Africans who were rich enough to afford the fees sent their children to boarding schools.

During week days, people worked from seven o'clock in the morning to around noon when they had one and a half hours of free time during the hottest part of the day. Most of the streets were empty at this time of day as people quietly found a place to escape the heat. During those week days Asian families were rarely seen; they remained behind the doors and fences of their compounds. But on Saturdays and especially Sundays when the town was almost clear of Africans, when the Africans were mostly at their homes and farms in the rural villages away from the towns, it was then that the East Indian women appeared, always attractively dressed in colorful saris and long beautiful dresses, leisurely walking and conversing in the town streets or entering the one movie house from which wafted the stirring music of a sitar. Their hair was done in long black strands and shone and gave off a perfume. Girls with long hair all nicely done and the boys in short khaki pants and shirts masterfully ironed by African servants came out of their homes and flooded streets and byways of entire towns.

They paraded up and down the streets, sat out in front of stores which were always closed on Sundays. The women greeted each other and exchanged the week's gossip. Children exchanged the news from their schools. Boys looked at older girls and talked sports. Girls seemed not to notice the boys, but they collected in groups under the jacaranda trees and whispered about the boys. The men sat or stood in small groups talking about the week's business and making new deals for the coming weeks.

If you strolled near the talking men, you heard names like Patel, Dias, or Adatia, and you heard talk about the sugar cane plantation or the cement factory or coffee trading or tea industry. If you came near women, there was talk of the children and school, of marriage, and of who had made a big coup in business or who had been promoted.

Most East Indian families ran some kind of business such as a small shop that sold tea, sugar, rice, beans, crackers, hair oil, combs, aspirin or flour, charcoal, cooking oil, kerosene, cooking pots, dishes, spoons, hoes, shovels, *pangas*. For important, well-paying jobs in the British services like those in the public works—water, roads, streets, traffic supervisors—East Indian men were made overseers. These jobs were given to East Indians rather than Africans. Men who worked these jobs found ways to make more money through making deals and charging people extra for getting jobs done quickly. People in these jobs could make money quickly and become rich. People who found work as teachers and low-level clerks were stuck with their salaries and did not have leverage to get ahead financially.

PEACE CORPS IN A REFUGEE CAMP

Soon after I came to Uganda, I met a group of Peace Corp recruits who spent several weeks assisting in a Watusi refugee camp. There were five women and six men between the ages of twenty-one and twenty-five: several recent high school graduates, an apprenticed carpenter, and college students interrupting their education to spend two years with the Corps in East Africa. I was teaching at Ntare School in Mbarara and curious about the rumors of the civil war in Rwanda, a neighboring country. Tall people streamed into town and filled the nearby camp in the Oruchinga Valley. During school holidays, I drove the ten miles to the camp in my Volkswagen with two female teachers from Bishop Stewart College.

In the distance, smoke rose from the camp fires and huts stretched over a wide hill and valley above a lake in a fertile area reclaimed from an infestation of tsetse fly. We were greeted by a British Red Cross nurse arriving a week earlier from a camp in the Congo. Sister Cecile was a Catholic nun, a former Mother Superior who preferred direct service in the refugee camps of Africa and India. She ran the camp with a staff of two refugee women and two male volunteers. After thirty minutes in her company, we were recruited as helpers. The two female teachers managed the milk hut, filling gourds for mothers with babies, and looked after the makeshift one-room nursery. A young girl refugee, now an apprentice nurse, learned techniques like sanitation and managing a kitchen which fed hundreds of hungry refugee children.

I distributed powdered milk, beans, cups of sugar, and rice to a line of refugees who had shelter but no food. An airlift of food from the USA and Britain had been delivered from Entebbe. We pitched in to help, but while working we despaired. We were too few and there was too much work to do. Sister persuaded us to stay several days, promising, "Help is on the way."

One night we woke to the bright lights and roar of motorcycle and Land Rover motors. People yelled, "Here they are! Hooray!"

I met Patrick, a tall, blonde, muscular guy, and Brian Murphy, a short swarthy one, and Bodice Richards, Lisa Nasaki, and several others. By first light, a wide tent was thrown up and spread like a white blossom above the group of eleven new arrivals sitting on camp chairs or reclining on mats, drinking tea and coffee, eating breakfast, looking all around, and laughing a lot.

Sister Cecile ordered several young males and two women to dig a pit along the hillside for disposal of food or wrappers.

"The ants will come, like they did in the Congo."

The next day Patrick, the carpenter, and Brian set a cement foundation and log beams for a two-room school. Later Patrick and Brian roofed the building while refugee teenagers handed up metal slabs. I helped some Tutsi men clear away stumps and flatten a new soccer field. We set eucalyptus tree trunks as goal posts.

Finally, Sister Cecile rested and drank tea. She planned to open a clinic and invite medics and doctors to set up special visiting days to treat chronic illness. Hammers rang; babies grew healthier; people made friends. Luganda and Congolese music blared from transistor radios while people danced and hugged. I was amazed by what a group of talented young Americans could do in that short time before Christmas.

Days passed with music and jokes among the Peace Corps workers. The nurses and refugees worried that the food, emptied cans, and dropped candy wrappers would attract the terrible Sifu, the soldier ants.

These busy American kids became favorites of the Tutsi refugees, moving among the children, learning words of the language, and mapping. The houses made by the Batutsi from grass, bamboo, and mud fascinated them. Some girls copied the native method of strapping babies on their backs. Others watched women cooking on open flames or practiced carrying trays of bananas or pineapples balanced on their heads with their hands free.

On Christmas Eve, the whole group invited themselves to a party at my house in Ntare School compound. Sister Cecile would not leave her camp even for a night. At the party, romances bloomed among the Peace Corp crew. They drank beer, sang Christmas songs, and expected to receive mail soon, posting them at schools and centers throughout Uganda. Two days after Christmas, when we returned to the refugee camp, some members had to leave to take up their posts. Patrick, Lisa, and Bodice and three others remained with us.

Several nights later we were awakened by loud screams from the Peace Corps tents. Patrick yelled, "What the hell is this?" Then several female voices followed, "Ow. It's here! Eou! Weee! Biting me on my legs!"

Candles and lanterns and strong flashlights came on. Somebody yelled, "The ants are everywhere!" Then they were running from the tents, beating the ground with blankets where long rows of the fierce insects ran.

Bodice was as usual taking care of the babies. Patrick and Lisa started a fire in the fire pit. "They sting like fire..." Patrick located the moving red ribbon of ants in his flashlight's glare, going toward the food pit. He flashed his lamp along the way and came down, stomping hard on them with his heavy shoes.

There was no more sleep. The Peace Corps men, using fire, grabbed their clothes and sheets, folded the tents, inspecting everything several times before putting them in the Land Rover. Patrick sat on the motorcycle, the motor running. There were only five of them left, and they had tea and biscuits, being careful where they dropped crumbs. Then they hugged Sister Cecile and briefly saluted the sleeping babies. Waving vigorously, the Peace Corps people, having already served, left the Oruchinga Refugee Camp for their postings across East Africa.

Place of the Lions

Africa is an exotic and beautiful place and, because of its natural beauty, the traveler is often forgetful of the imminent and constant dangers.

I served in Uganda about nine of the ten years that I was in Africa, and I married and bought a *shamba* in Ankole, on which I helped to build a three-room mud house with cement floors. It was fortified with strong doors. My wife and two children lived there, close by a county chief's family. At night all kinds of creatures visited us. Lions roared, big cats ate our goats. Along with a farm worker, I once clubbed and captured a civet foraging in our chicken shack.

One day, with the sun blaring down on our yard, my four-year-old son Ngoma wandered outside into the yard carrying his lunch sandwich. A large hawk-like bird swooped quickly and furiously from the sky down, and before my eyes took the sandwich out of Ngoma's hands. I was frightened: the fast-moving, windy whisk and beating rush of the wings, the quick violent swoop must have injured the boy. But Ngoma stood before me, holding his undamaged arms up, hands out into the air, gazing in awe into the sky after the retreating bird. The encounter had not bruised or scratched the skin of his arms.

Over the hills, a short distance from our house in Ankole, long lines of villagers of all ages gathered at a borehole, pumping and filling their pots with water. I think we had all attached almost no meaning to the place name, Wonchunchu, which in Runyankore means "place of the lions," a name given in olden times. Apparently, the lions had not forgotten, for villagers often lost lambs and goats to lions.

One day, not knowing the meaning of the name, I went for a walk in those *murram* hills. The hills were steep, speckled with caves, stunted bush, and isolated mesas. Before I knew it, I was no longer meeting people. I was alone; no goat boys chasing their goats or playing flutes met me. I stopped in the shadows of a clump of trees to wipe sweat from my hot face. A soft wind blew toward me, and I looked under a copse of trees in a *murram* half-cave and saw this tawny figure reclining. At first I was not sure, but then I became aware of the rising and falling of its body...breathing. The large head and flowing mane shocked me. I stood momentarily disoriented. Frozen for an instant, I was unable to move. Yes, it was a lion!

I am surprised now that I did not panic and run away, which might have fatally drawn the lion's attention to me, a rushing, moving prey. Quietly but hurriedly I slipped away in the direction from which I had come, and soon I was panting but meeting goat herders and hiking villagers again. I shivered in fear and wonder of what would have happened had the wind from me been blowing toward the lion instead of the wind blowing from the lion to me. It could have revealed to the lion my scent, and things might have been far different in the "Place of the Lions."

THE SNAKES

When I bought a small farm in Ankole, Uganda, I experienced the problem of shortage of fresh water. There was a bore hole fitted with a pump nearby, but we needed more water right near the house.

I tried to solve our water problem by buying a five-hundred-gallon metal tank, placing it beside the house, and running gutters from the roof of the house to catch the run-off water. During the rainy season, this gave a great supply of water. But lizards skittered over the corrugated roof and dropped waste, contaminate the water, limiting its use to irrigating our garden or washing floors and work clothes.

With that failure, I turned to digging a well, since we lived on a hillside and the water table was relatively high. In preparation for cementing around our well, I brought in several loads of sand and piled it alongside the drive way to the house. During rainy season, the grass grew out, covering the tall mounds of sand. Animals migrated from the low areas to our hillside. We had more partridge nests in the grass and weaver birds in the acacias. We never thought what happened to other animals from the low areas.

By this time I had one small son, and there were three other nieces and nephews of my wife's relatives visiting us and playing in the grass around the yard. I came from my teaching job in Kampala to spend the weekend with my family where my wife, in early pregnancy with our second child, was remaining to oversee a hired person putting in a garden for the coming short rainy season, just a month away.

On Sunday, I prepared to head back from our house to work a week. While loading my car, I spied the mounds of sand with grass growing out of them. I remembered then how the children played in the newly dumped sand during the dry season. Now the grasses covered the sand. With the grass-cutting blade, I took a few swings at the grass just to give the hired man a hint. I wanted all the grass cut away from the house.

With a swing of the blade, my eye caught a sudden twinkle of movement in the grass. I brought a hoe and struck it down into the sand and pulled. Along with the emerging blade came the twisting brown, gray, and yellow body of a snake. The hoe had sliced it almost in half, near the middle of the body. Now it moved menacingly, twisting toward me on the cut stalks of green grass. All the while, the snake kept twisting its head, baring its fangs, striking the hoe. I struck the head several times and everyone from the house gathered nearby, frightened.

We reviewed the possibilities: what might have happened had the children played in the grass on that mound of sand? I observed the snake. Its diamond head and its coloring told me it was poisonous. I had no doubt: it was a pit viper. But then I remembered that these snakes usually came in pairs, and so wondered if there might be another or even several more in these sand piles. I did not have far to look.

I began moving the sand with the hoe. Soon a second viper rose up quickly and attacked the hoe handle, striking it numerous times with its head, moving back and forth, sending fangs into the lower hoe handle. I dropped the hoe in panic and went for a nearby stick and attacked the snake with it.

The whole family came outside the house and quietly watched the snake and me. I feared the snake, and at the same time feared for my family's safety if there were other snakes around. I finally dispatched the second snake.

I searched through the piles of sand and found a nest of mice in one sand pile, housed in gathered leaves, but no more snakes. All grass and weeds were cleared away from the sand piles, the house, and its driveway, clear to our newly made outhouse.

We learned a lesson and made a rule to watch carefully for snakes, and no one should venture out of the house after dark. I am sure that lesson learned from our encounter with the snakes that morning, and the vigilance we exercised afterwards saved us from snake bites.

The Ndulu

I don't know if actual justice is quick and final in Africa, but I have witnessed the brevity and finality of judgments associated with ideas of justice and the Ndulu with its almost instantaneous dispensations.

I was at an open air market in the countryside in Uganda. At these markets people crowd the highway before daybreak, coming for miles with trussed chickens, stalks of maize, bunches of bananas, sacks of beans, riding on bicycles, motor scooters, cars, trucks, or walking with bundles of all types, babies and baskets on their heads, swaying as they walk for miles.

At the market, goods are spread out in rows. There are a few sheds and buildings and trees for shade, but most of the goods are laid out in rows for miles on the flat green earth. They sit on sacks and blankets and bedsteads which are also sold.

These markets go on for days. Some people put down blankets and sleep on them at night. I have never noticed a policeman or any kind of law enforcement officer, although there are county chiefs called Gombolas who allot space and collect government taxes from the sellers.

One Saturday afternoon we attended one of these markets with a group of boys from the school after a soccer match at a nearby village. The schoolboys were busy spending their allowances on tooth-cleaning sticks, knitted handkerchiefs, and soap and hair brushes when a cry went up from the far reaches of the market. Everyone stopped and stood at rapt attention to listen.

"Shall we be off, sir?" one boy said with fear in his voice.

I noticed another boy picking up a sharp rock. He was from this place and said, "It's the Ndulu, signaling...a thief...or murderer...or something more." Somebody was in trouble. There was that horrible sound again. It went through the whole of the market: a terrifying, wrenching herald of trouble.

I learned about it later on. The Ndulu is a signal of serious trouble. It's a call to attention for everyone far and near who could hear the voice. The alarmist put up his head and made the deadly horrifying sound from his mouth as loud as he could, with his open palm vibrating in front of his mouth. Over his lips it sounded: "*Nululululu ohlu ou ndulluoohho; luuu ouuluu,*" and kept going until people joined the caller. There nearby, being pointed out, was the accused, a thief, a murderer, an offender; it was very serious wrong, something the village did not tolerate.

On the day of that Ndulu in the Saturday market, there stood on barren ground near the market a young man in shorts, naked to the waist. Whatever he had stolen—or was accused of stealing—was no longer with him. It was discarded, hurriedly, thrown in a pile on the ground nearby: someone's goods, an open bag of collected pilfered jewelry, a watch, a ring.

It was clear to everyone that he was a thief, now tied with ropes and vines. They held their pilloried victim to a big eucalyptus post near two tethered goats also waiting for slaughter. His hands were raised and head bowed in mercy supplications.

People pointed accusing fingers at him and spat accusations: "Thief. Liar. Sneak! I hate you!" A number of people who came fists closed tight over rocks. Everyone hurled threats and accusations his way. No one defended him. He had no friends in this crowd.

Then it began. Rocks flew through the air from every quarter. The crowd of people swelled, and the volume and volleys of rocks hitting the man was a heavy rain, causing him to shrink, lose his rigidity and sink to the ground until he was a tattered, bleeding heap attached loosely by vines that held what was left of the former breathing, human that we had all seen and heard pleading before the rain of hard stone hit him.

Then a silence! Not a sound... Everyone slowly turned from what had been him... the human, now a tattered thing... Him!

And slowly they went back to their duties in the market, and all voices were silent until slowly there raised a din of sounds as if nature had turned up a volume button. We heard again the sounds of people hawking their wares: "*Matoke!*" "Baked yams!" and chickens and cassava. Meanwhile, over the shoulder you saw the burial unit wrapped the mass of the thief in banana leaves with other waste, garbage, in branches and old rags, and carted it away in a wheelbarrow.

I thought how swift and final was the judgment brought on by the Ndulu against that man. No time in jail, no relatives spending long anguished days and years. All quickly finished. And final.

FIELD TRIP: KAMPALA TO MOMBASA

At the city bar in Kampala, Gene Ashby and I made our radical decision over drinks. It was better to teach marine biology on the beach in Mombasa amid the remnants of East African colonialism across the road from Lord Delaware's Plantation outside of Nairobi than to teach those subjects from books and pictures in our classrooms.

We thought it such a great idea that we petitioned old Porskitt, our headmaster at Kyambogo Teacher Training College, to allow us to go on a field trip by bus to Mombasa with forty students, males and females.

We thought he would "freak out." But as he gazed at us through those thick eyeglasses; his eyes became gleeful and young. Instead of rejecting us, he said, "That's the spirit we need around here." He helped us plan the trip by calling headmasters at other schools to feed our students and put us up for the night when we passed through their area.

We secured a bus and two drivers. For further security, one of us drove my old beat-up Datsun in case we had bus trouble and needed to go to the nearest town for a mechanic.

At the end of term, our field trip began—with disciplined, self-controlled teacher trainees who were twenty to twenty-five years old. Some were married; most had never before traveled this far outside their communities.

Our first stop was at the Owen Falls Dam at Jinja, where we toured the sugar and cement factories. From there, we hastened over a smooth tarmac road to Tororo Girls School near the Kenyan border where we spent our first night's lodging.

We crossed into Kenya in the early morning. The bus droned on, passing white and black rhinoceroses. Among the flat-topped mimosa we caught glimpses of reticulated giraffes. We made good time; soon we passed Eldoret and by late afternoon we were approaching Nakuru.

This was a talented group of trainees. With this leisure of travel, they showed many sides of creativity. Some were phenomenal musicians on drums or stringed lyres. Others drew or painted pictures and hung them throughout the bus. Several took on the task of writing a journal of our field trip. At intervals, they read portions of their compositions to the rapt attention of the whole group. Our women students decorated their half of the bus with silks and colorful scarves. Odors of perfumes and powders drifted from it through the rest of the bus.

We arrived early evening near the alkaline Lake Nakuru, and we saw white birds sitting as if on tables in the foliage of green, flat-topped trees. Birds flew up in droves—grebes, cranes, nightjars, noisy yellow weaver birds, many kinds of starlings—whirling and wheeling around in the blue sky above the trees and hills; very eye-catching and interesting.

But nothing rivaled the myriad masses of pink and red flamingoes feeding and ruffling up and down on the shores and even in the middle of the lake. The flamingoes flew up, marched along the lake ends, fed in the shallows, standing erect, their beaks on their long necks upside down, siphoning and filtering food into their bodies. All the while their feathers ruffled displaying the fuchsia and red plumage fueled by the algae and shrimp they ate from this alkaline lake water.

We spent the night at a secondary school near Lake Nakuru. Then quickly, in the morning, packed and boarded our bus with sleep still in our eyes. We passed a hill overlooking the lake. The moaning drone of our bus motor disturbed the nesting flamingoes. Frightened, they rose up in flocks. Soft, whispering waves of flamingoes, flaring wings floating upward from Lake Nakuru, through sparse green tree tresses in the early morning mist, looking like a sparkling pink veil floating in the sky over our yellow bus.

The scenery captured our eyes. Books, magazines and newspapers, lay about, but not many were opened. I remember many titles:

> Weep Not, Child
> Living in the Village of Ghosts
> Things Fall Apart
> Gone with the Wind

More books lay on a poster that read "When Elephants Fight it is the Grass that Suffers":

> Cry the Beloved Country
> Great Expectations
> The American Constitution
> Tom Brown's School Days

From here, the bus raced around curve after curve and up and down hill. Relaxing students slept or swayed up and down the aisles with the moving, droning bus, visiting with each other in their seats, laughing, exchanging jokes. The drivers, good humored and cooperative, knew the road and good naturedly coaxed us to stop at outdoor cafes that had food, beer, soft drinks, and latrines.

When we passed one town by, there was soon another, with roads always crowded with people headed to the next nearest town, loaded with baskets of maize, cassava, bananas, pineapples, sorghum, gourds of honey; there were bicycles loaded with sacks of beans or a person, a woman or child perched on the back carriage seat or riding in the handlebars of the bicycle or a motor scooter. No matter where we passed in the afternoon, there were these crowds headed back in the opposite direction.

Then five miles before we reached Nairobi, our luck changed; we had punctures in two rear tires. Latria Semakula (the women students' matron), Gene Ashby, and I held a brief staff meeting in the Datsun.

I was in charge of discipline, so in the end I was stuck with the bus. Gene loved to drink, so it was best he went with the drivers for mechanics and supervised some of the trainees who wanted to hike or hitch rides into Nairobi. He drove some students in our Datsun; others hiked or caught local buses and taxis to town to see the sights of Nairobi, promising to meet up with Gene at the post office. I stayed with Latria and most of the girls until the drivers and the garage repairmen came. They slowly, but expertly, in about six hours, repaired our bus tires.

When Gene and the last of the students finally dribbled back, we went to our host school in the hills above Nairobi. We were up in the hills in a school, a good distance from town where people were dancing in the bright lighted bars of Nairobi where our students really wanted to be. However, when we arrived at the host school, the young students there were having a dance and no one wanted to go to bed. After a while, our trainees all began dancing, having fun right there.

Early the next morning we went through Nairobi without stopping after Gene promised the students he would bring them back. It was early afternoon when our bus reached the outskirts of Mombasa. The drivers pulled to the side, out of traffic, to give the trainees a view of the entry. Cameras clicked amid students' shouts expressing excitement and joy when they saw the four big tusks that marked the entrance to Mombasa.

Students became impatient as our drivers searched for our school quarters along the length of spacious beaches. After being attracted by the many tourist hotels and camps along the beautiful white sandy beach, we finally located our school and unloaded our bags. Wearing skimpy shorts and barefooted, we headed for the beach. We all gathered there, happily dipping our toes into warm ocean water.

I expected the students to don bathing suits and head for the water. But only Mudede and Geld Patel and several others dove in and swam a ways out, shouting and throwing handfuls of water toward those on the beach who were not enticed to join them. Others walked along the sandy beach, sat under palm trees, joked about the many crabs, especially the hermit crabs which they collected, observed, and called "homeless" ones because they were always searching for a new home.

Only four students were keen to learn goggling and snorkeling, so we found the beach rental kiosk and rented equipment. All we could do that first evening was get used to the process of putting on the equipment. The students spat out the salt water. We could not collect any specimens, because we had neither container nor preservative.

The next morning, four students who wanted to snorkel came with me in the Datsun into Mombasa town to find a chemical warehouse where we bought formaldehyde and a large 100-gallon garbage can-type plastic container to hold our specimens. I ordered ready-made preservative in gallon jugs. That was easy, because I'd learned there were "collectors" operating along the beach, securing specimens for biological supply houses in England and Germany.

On our first day of collecting, a young German University student on holiday collecting specimens popped out of the water near us, in goggles and a snorkeling outfit, with a plastic collecting bag slung over his shoulder. He soon made friends with my crew, pointing out a small fish with spines he told us to take care not to touch or step on, because it was poisonous. He told us that he worked with his father during holidays collecting specimens for sale to a laboratory back home in Frankfurt, Germany.

Every low tide I combed the beach for specimens and shells, and made notes about them. While collecting with students, I taught them and made notes about their questions that I planned to include in my lessons back at the college.

Our German University student joined us frequently and was very useful in sharing information about collecting. He informed us that there was no danger of sharks because the coral reef came up too high. As long as we did not venture out beyond the barrier, there was no danger. That information relieved the fears of other students who soon joined us in swimming out to look or collecting and writing in notebooks. Our artists drew pictures daily.

Our group established a routine. I goggled and snorkeled with four and sometimes as many as eight of the teacher trainees and the collector from Germany. Meanwhile Gene took field trips with a large cadre of teacher trainees as far as Nairobi, to parliament to see Jomo Kenyatta and to see the big colonial plantations of Lord Delaware, the horse farms, and the air field. He told any listener that he was a social studies teacher back at the college and had finally thought how he could enrich and enliven his courses. The students wanted to make sure they learned something of the colonial experience of Kenyans. Uganda was never a colony and was spared that colonial past; it was a protectorate during colonial times, when England ruled through the chiefs and kings they found already in Uganda.

With these established routines, we had meals in the school and on the beach, and we spent quiet evenings reading, writing, reflecting, cataloging, and preserving our specimens. We met every evening to sight-see, visiting the forts and historical sites along the beach.

Gradually students filled our plastic collection container. More and more of our number cultivated visits to the beach. Mrs. Semakula had most of the girls in bathing suits, where they often frolicked in the water during the siesta period; a time when the beach was free of fishermen and collectors.

Our week slipped away day by fast-moving day.

Then it was gone, and we left Mombasa with our collection utensil full and headed over the long road through Kenya.

Leaving Mombasa behind us, the teacher trainees slept, recounted their adventures, or quietly wrote in their journals. We quickly passed Nairobi, stopping at our host schools on the way, but now hurrying back to Kyambogo University in Kampala.

We arrived on a quiet, seemingly deserted campus late one night; school was still on holiday. It would be several weeks before staff and students would savor our adventure when we reported at a special assembly or taught our newly acquired knowledge to newly arrived students.

And now, still, years after, in a protected corner of the Science Laboratory at Kyambogo University, which was formerly Kyambogo Teacher Training College, is a one-hundred-gallon reinforced hard plastic container of marine animals and plants preserved in formaldehyde and alcohol: starfishes, octopus, crabs, oysters, clams, seaweeds, puffer fish, hermit crabs, limpets, sand fleas, and algae-kelp, varied and sundry of marine specimens we collected on that field trip taken with forty teacher trainees from Kyambogo to Mombasa.

This collection forms the physical lab parts of an introductory course in marine biology that the present science staff offers to the teacher trainees in landlocked Uganda. Teaching social studies is not much changed. The teachers still use maps and pictures, but videos make lessons more interesting and up to date.

Flash Photos of a Tyrant Rising

1. Early Days

Idi Amin Dada was born in Koboko, West Nile, in 1925. He had very little formal education. He joined the King's African Rifles (KAR) in 1946, and was a rough field soldier with the KAR before independence in 1962.

Amin is the favorite of high and low British officers: They love his desire to please, and his exertions and efforts to secure whatever they desire, such as women, drink, cheap goods, and illicit companionship.

His dressing description: Untidy dresser—pants too tight, shirts bulging out of trousers, total uniform never fitting properly.

Amin's persona: Huge body, bulging muscles, big face, enormous smiling mouth with large white teeth.

Mannerisms: Playful, cruel but gets along well with fellow soldiers.

Amin as a boxer is always looking for a way to advance. Fights for the attention of the audience.

Knows how to put on a show, pleasing would-be friends by unmercifully smashing opponents...while himself laughing.

2. THE BOXER

"Amin is a big burly boxer who won bouts at the European club in Nairobi and Kampala."

He is asked by British officers to remain after bouts in the non-integrated European club for drinks and jokes, and he allows them to feel his big muscles.

He is the central favorite of some when drinking. They tell off-color jokes about him, in his presence.

As a boxer, he crushes and humiliates opponents—Africans from other tribes. He uses these cruel tactics to get promoted to sergeant.

He takes suggestions from superiors that make his uniforms neater. He begins to have his clothes tailored to fit. His decoration ribbons for boxing and marksmanship are worn smartly across his huge chest.

3. OFFICERS NEEDED

He speaks with his officers about education deficits. He answers with boxing exploits: "Bring somebody to challenge me."

They bet money on bouts and win big.

Amin crushes opponents and earns big purses for officers.

They talk about his education. "Nothing positive there!"

Another British commander talks of "leaving the bloody KAR," because there will be no future after independence: "It's an army of blacks." The KAR needs African officers.

"None of the blokes are trained." In conversation they consider Amin as officer material, but his educational level deters them. He went only as far as to senior 1? Not even verifiable records there.

4. NO HARM DONE

The British officers need someone to leave in charge of the KAR units. They need someone with training. They have a meeting, drink and talk of Idi Amin.

They give him a kind of half-fun ethics test of what-ifs. He fails, miserably, but they vote to send him for training in the UK.

They voice the opinion that training and association in the military academy will somehow rub off his rough edges. In connection with this, they complain of the soft African University-trained officers above him.

Will they keep him in check, bring him along, bring him up through the ranks in time?

Their ambitious maneuvering will keep him in check. Moreover: "It's a lark," and "We know he will fail in the elite military academy." They feel that there's no harm done in their attitude.

5. IN THE RIGHT PLACE

Does everything up to standard at the military academy. Observes. Surprises everyone concerned.

He has learned his military manners, knows ordinary field ordinance and protocol for officers and enlisted men.

They consistently waive his education requirements. They note that he has no training in ethics or psychology, but yet vote to send him to a higher military school. The need for African officers in the KAR is crucial.

They get notes from field officers who say they are badly in need of officers who know major weapon systems as well as vehicles and troop positioning. They should have the training that other African countries have provided their officers, which they have previously neglected in Uganda's KAR.

He is in the right place. They send him on extended visits to top military academies to prep him for advancement.

6. INTO CONGO

He receives the full knowledge and capability of military ordnance without knowledge of ethical requirements to that level and type of training.

He returns to Uganda and is sent into combat in the Congo as an officer.

Rumors float of discord between President Obote and General Amin.

Gold and diamonds disappear from coffers where the president and his generals are dealing with the Congo. Whispers about Amin being implicated.

7. RUMORS

News report of Amin having slipped away for a secret meeting with Gaddafi in Libya.

That he signed a secret deal.

Overhead every day there is a lot of activity. Fast fighter planes zooming loud and low through the sky over Kampala.

Pilots from Israel are training Ugandan pilots.

There is a picture in the *Uganda Argus* showing pilots with their instructors.

President Obote prepares to attend a Commonwealth Conference. People say the president should not absent himself at this time.

8. DISFAVOR

There is a shake-up in the military ranks.

Amin is passed over for promotion while other senior officers are elevated over and beyond him.

New high-ranking officers are without battalions but are now in charge of the army.

Common rumor: Amin is in disfavor.

President Obote leaves for the trip to the Commonwealth Conference.

Amin shows up at Makerere University graduation exercises, standing in full military attire. We are all wearing academic regalia. He is totally alone. No one approaches him. He is without his honor unit.

9. TERRIBLE THINGS

Reports by Uganda Television and *Uganda Argus*:

Generals and their wives are killed in the north.

Rumors and questions:

> Will the president return from the Commonwealth Conference?
> Who is in charge now?

No answer.

The coup sirens sound through the night.

Gunfire sounds far and near.

Loud joyous shouting in the streets and roadways amid loud shrieks of gunfire and zooming vehicles on the roadway below Kyamboga.

Some are hiding in fear in their houses under beds.

From a Kyamboga school building, we watch.

I see terrible things.

Later I am face down in the *murram* dirt with gun barrels very near overhead.

These were not distant happenings at all.

10. ALL IS CONFUSED

Rumor: there has been a coup.

Unanswered questions: What about the president? Will he return? Was he killed abroad?

Soldiers—"regular by their uniforms"—are seen fleeing uphill near the college across the road near a reservoir. They throw off their uniforms and fling away their weapons, their guns, among the cassava plants. Some servants sneak down and retrieve weapons, then disappear in the nearby forest.

11. CHECKPOINTS

Next day on TV it is announced that the CID chief is missing.

His wife and family are still at Kyamboga in the house opposite mine. His talented children in the yard are banging on drums and blowing on make-believe horns.

On the roads, checkpoints are set up at all roundabouts.

Soldiers are commandeering Mulago Hospital medical transport vehicles and agriculture vehicles for transport of large groups of soldiers who hang from the sides of vehicles—with guns. They rush to checkpoints through town and countryside.

People report seeing bodies.

Schools are on holiday as the country holds its breath.

12. POWER SHIFTS

Then on Uganda Television two nights later, the murky water clears.

There is the new president doing his duty: General Idi Amin Dada, interviewing Mr. Oryema, Inspector General of Police.

Another coup: The criminal interviewing the police chief.

The police chief is under klieg lights squirming and sweating trying to say the "right" answers to his "crime" of not arresting the killers of the generals in that northern city.

Mr. Oryema tries to appear not guilty of the crime committed by the generals. And he tries not to say the truth. But his condition—his unconditional surrender to his questioner—is apparent. He demonstrates his powerlessness.

Should it be the other way around?

The head of the CID is now dead.

The county holds its breath! The rest is...Horrible!

SUTTEE AND CHANDRA

Mr. Chandra was a slender man whose face was that light brown color of Hindi boiled tea with milk. His wife was a slight shade lighter and tended her profile in every mirror with which she became acquainted. Semidry Chandra loved books and ideas. He had always been a success in school and in the world of ideas. Privately he took pride in being a teacher. He did not like being a trader. In the early years of his marriage to Lila Vital, he had tried a small shop in Fiji. Lila was a beautiful but uneducated girl who longed to be rich and listened to the schemes of other women who spoke of how clever their husbands were and told of deals that brought their families riches. The daughters of these women went about on parade Sundays in fine clothes after wearing drab green school uniforms all week, while the Chandra daughters wore dresses quickly sewn from cheap but colorful cloth bought by their mother at a higher price in one of the high-end shops.

For a short time Lila had cut and sold bolts of expensive colorful cloth and cheap glittering jewelry. Though Lila loved the shop and the status it gave, she had no head for business and keeping records. And Mr. Chandra worked even harder, studying in the schools wherever they went and viewing teaching as the chosen way for his family to hold on to the tenuous level of affluence he had attained. He applied himself, hoping Lila would forget grandiose ideas of riches and settle for a steady, hard grind of study to upgrade herself as well. The students chastised her and loved and admired her teacher husband. They talked of the couple often, praising the husband and wondering at the wife's unhappiness. My students showed their affection for Mr. Chandra, who was head of the science department at the college where we taught.

He and I shared an office, and I heard snatches of conversation between them when his wife visited him while we worked. Her talk was all about opening businesses, which she tried over and over. Each time, as she complained, it was no fault of her own that she failed and lost whatever money they had invested. The students would come to class whispering: "Mrs. Chandra's new shop had just closed." Again and again he told her she did not have the temperament for business: "We care too much about people to succeed in business."

He reminded her of other ventures. "Remember in Fiji, in your shop there: when you let out cloth on credit to those women who made dresses for their daughters and then couldn't pay. You let them off. You are learning over and over that business is not friendship. You mix them and you lose."

"So I must sit and do nothing."

"No, just know it is better to keep a small shop with gum and candy, coffee and aspirins. No involved expense and bookkeeping."

"But that does not give the big return of cloth and expensive jewelry."

"It is true it does not give the big losses either."

But after a time, he supported her in another shop. And soon after it was rumored they could not pay the landlord the rent on their living compound. Mr. Chandra was seen driving a tractor at night, doing road-clearing work.

One Hindi student said, "She's out of control. My grandma said in other times the village women would watch her."

"Watch her?" I said, over the test tubes in science class.

"Yes, she is putting the family in danger."

I did not know what possible danger. "What do they mean?"

"That is far in other times," Dalken said.

"I know he's thinking if anything happens, she will be responsible. "

"But it is not allowed anymore. That's why she is pushing him so hard. She wants her way."

So it went until his wife became adamant. So Mr. Chandra gave in and let her once again open a shop that quickly failed.

It was customary for our science students to have tea one day a week as a kind of review seminar where students asked questions and discussed difficult topics. The students came to tea one day. Mr. Chandra was not yet there, but they said he was closing his wife's shop. He did not show during the afternoon, so when classes ended for the day, I closed the lab office and went home.

The next morning when I arrived at the lab, I was met by the custodian. He emerged from the office wringing his hands, a dreaded look of horror on his face. I saw beyond him into the office. The headmaster and several other staff members were shaking their heads as they contemplated a body stretched out beyond them on the floor. Beside an overturned chair, a chemical bottle lay open with some of its contents spilled about and a spoon nearby. And there was Mr. Chandra lying dead, his body all contorted.

The headmaster, a grey-haired man from Britain, closed the lab and with several assistants waited for the police and talked with them in the closed lab for an hour. He dismissed us and announced to the student body that the school was closed for two days, that there had been a terrible incident that had taken Mr. Chandra away from us and we would get the official details later.

But the news was all over the campus: Mr. Chandra had committed suicide by taking spoonsful of a mercury compound. My students whispered it was his wife's fault. The students mulled about in mixed groups around the teachers' college campus. Usually the students hung about in isolated ethnic groups, but now they mixed,

African and Asian students, talking together, trying to make sense of what had happened.

Asian students from my science class congregated on the green near my house and chatted. I also wanted to know what had happened. Phrases they had uttered in class now needed an explanation. I invited them in for tea. The girls got out the tea things, and the boys talked among themselves. One said Mr. Chandra was very smart, but he had behaved stupidly; first, for not controlling his wife's behavior, and, second, for doing harm to himself.

But the girl who made tea said it was the wife's fault. "He was a man of principle. My grandpa says at home, he knows the part of India where Mrs. Chandra came from, and he knows they practiced it."

"Practiced what?" I wanted to know.

"When a husband died like this, what a wife must do."

Another said, "But that was long ago. It's now against the law. But my grandpa knows, knows Mr. Chandra loved knowledge and teaching, and his wife loved money and she goaded him. She didn't like him to be a teacher. She wanted him to make money so she could be rich and show how important she was. And everyone had better watch her, because my grandmother said, 'She will show her feelings after the ceremony.'"

"Yes, only my grandpa said, 'But not her; she doesn't even care he's gone.'"

"But she has to care," said Desai.

"But why must she be watched?" I asked.

Several students started to answer, saying, "The ceremony. You know they cremate him. Maybe...that's when...probably tomorrow."

The girl making tea said, "But my grandpa says that part is long over; it is outlawed. They cannot do it anymore. It's long since over. But if a wife is so saddened, she might..."

A silent girl pulled her sari scarf around her head and then spoke. "You all should not talk of it. She might do it. That's why she should be watched."

One day later, in the early afternoon, Bosni and Peak Patel knocked on my door.

"Sir, the others said you wanted to see."

"See?" I said.

"You know the ceremony of Mr. Chandra, sir."

I knew then he meant the cremation. "Where?"

"You come with us. It's at the edge of town, on a little-used road where no one travels."

We left the campus main road, walking through forest and weeds, and came to a place where there was a little-used path on the edge of the forest, high above the streets of town. The isolated road abutted an abandoned lumber truckway that washed out during heavy rains, with ruts and deep gullies, one not used by regular traffic. To the side of the road was a wooden trailer on tractor tires, the kind of trailer you see on the road usually pulled behind trucks or cars carrying loads of furniture or heavy machinery or old tires. Now it was loaded with a mixture of stacked cords of wood, old truck tires, and dry bales of hay, stacked very high with an empty space in the center.

An open truck with many colored streamers arrived among the waiting men, and as they removed the body and put it in the center of the loaded trailer, the crowd swelled and people covered the hillside. We were behind it all at the edge of the woods, but we heard constant chanting from the crowd as the flames rose, spreading until the whole trailer was engulfed. People stood some distance away. Even though it was late in the afternoon, the African sun was still hot.

Bosni and Patel recognized some of the people from town, and some teachers were there, but there was no sign of Mrs. Chandra. Maybe they detained her at home. Then they spotted an entourage of women standing away, nearer the road, watching the flaming pyre. Bosni said, "She's there. I see her there." He nodded to point the direction. "They have her surrounded."

We waited in our cover while the flames leaped, burned, and the odor of burning rubber assailed our nostrils, and the whole wooden trailer and tires with the body was consumed.

"What did they expect might happen?" I wondered out loud.

Patel said, "Well, in other times, if a woman had driven her husband to ruin...I mean...in the old India, during cremation...a woman...a wife would dash from among the watchers and throw herself upon the burning pyre and perish on her husband's body."

"That's not done anymore," Bosni hastened to put in.

"No, the British colonialists forbade it. Put a stop to it. But even now, every now and then throughout the world where Indian women are, some woman tries to save face by doing it."

"But not Mrs. Chandra," the girl with the colorful sari said. "I heard she is going to Nairobi where she has relatives."

In the following weeks, in class the students spoke of Mrs. Chandra leaving with her daughters on the train, going to relatives in Nairobi.

I BECOME AN AFRICAN FARMER

In 1965, I had been in Uganda four years. I was married to a Tutsi woman and had one child, with a second child on the way. One evening after tea, one of my science students brought to me an African woman whose father was a county chief in Ankole. She offered to sell me twelve acres of her land. It was too much land for me. Besides, I was not a citizen and the law stated that only Ugandan citizens could own land.

This land-owning woman encouraged me in every way to purchase it. She was, I now think, an early-era African feminist. She said, "Since you're married to an African woman and have children, then why not buy the land for your wife and children?" At her urging, I investigated land ownership law at the land office and found that it was legal for me to purchase land in my wife's name.

I bought the land. It was surveyed and put in my wife's name along with the child's name. I put on a caveat that restricted the sale of it until the child reached the age of twenty-one. This pleased the seller very much.

It was my intention to make sure the land offered a safeguard of care for the mother and child. I was looking ahead, thinking of the welfare of the child and mother in case something unforeseen happened to me, or in case she decided to divorce me and marry another man. There was the possibility that I might not be around and without the caveat, the land could be sold, and without that land, the child could be left with no means of care.

My students heard I had bought land, and they came to visit me with large eyes of expectancy. They said, "Sir, what will you do now?" It was a question that said I was in some kind of trouble.

I heard one student say, "...but he is the son of farmers in Mississippi."

The other's retort followed: "But this is Africa. Can he farm *matoke*? Can he grow cassava?"

That was more like a dare. It rattled my thinking just a bit.

That is the beginning of how I acquired land in Uganda and slowly became an African farmer. I thought I could at least grow beans and tomatoes in Ankole.

In preparation for planting, I hired a local farmer's helper to make a potting shed, roofed it with grass roofing, and made benches for the wooden trays in which I had about four inches of soil. I planted beans, corn, squash, tomatoes, and peppers. My students asked, "What is that for, sir?" None of the nearby farmers had a potting shed. And I was just doing what I had seen done back in Mississippi.

Other African farmers in our village of Kaberere, which was about eight miles from the town of Mbarara and Nymatangia Catholic Mission, came to visit often and offered advice. "Pay attention to the rainy season," one warned me.

Further, I made use of the British government's Experimental Stock Farm near Mbarara, which was still in operation just three years after Uganda became independent. At the stock farm, African farmers got farms started by purchasing baby chickens and pigs and by hiring at a nominal fee heavy farm-machines for tilling and plowing. I hired the plowing of two acres and immediately planted beans, yams, and peanuts.

I tried to solve the water problem by buying a large five-hundred-gallon metal tank. I placed it beside the house to collect the roof runoff during rains. At first I thought to use it as drinking water. I found lizards skittering over the corrugated roof and birds dropping their feces on the roof, and all this drained into the tank, contaminating the water. The water could be safely used only for washing work clothes or for scrubbing our cement floors. But the tank was now almost full of rain water.

I went back to teaching at Kyambogo in Kampala, and in my absence I forgot to transplant my tomato and pepper plants from the potting shed where they were still growing, cared for by my wife and my farm-helper.

Upon my return to my farm, the neighboring farmers warned me that the rainy season was over and I could not transplant my tomatoes. The searing sun would shrivel and kill them. It was now the dry season, and we were harvesting beans and corn. I was disappointed, but still I went ahead and transplanted two long rows of tomato plants from the potting shed.

In three days, they lay shriveled and parched, and then died. Nearby farmers came, looked at them sadly, and shook their heads in pity. My schoolboy students said, "Sir, this is Africa!" as though they reminded me that I must not act like I was still in Mississippi.

But then I thought there should be a way to grow these tomato plants. So at night, I thought of a possible way to protect my plants from the searing rays of the sun. I dug a deeper hole for each plant, and at night I transplanted more and covered all around the stems at the top of their roots with grass and banana fibers. My farmer friends watched, smiled, and shrugged their shoulders as if they expected failure. Then each night I took a bucket filled with water and poured water from my big tank into each hill around the roots and covered around the base of each plant with more grass.

The next days, I watched the plants carefully. They did not wilt, and after a week of pouring water from my big corrugated tank the tomato plants were green and still healthy in the hot sun. They were growing taller and taller.

My neighbor farmers came to look, and they raised their eyes in surprise, clearly mystified that my tomato plants were healthy.

They saw my family visiting the bore hole for drinking and cooking water.

I finally told my farmer friends the secret of my mulching and watering the plants at night from water in my tank.

From then on, they visited me often and soon the tomato plants bloomed, and there were small tomatoes that kept on enlarging and all during the dry season they grew, and we had plants loaded with tomatoes as large as tea cups. My neighbors became more interested. We talked about mulching as a way of having plants grow during the dry season. They visited and went home with several huge tomatoes.

We all knew then that we could plant during dry season if we solved the water problem.

SUNDOWNER

Sometimes personal items left in odd places can lead to humor, romance, or mayhem. When I first arrived in Kampala at Kyambogo Teacher Training College, I was assigned a house in the usual way that teaching masters are housed when they arrive on school compounds. The house assigned me had recently been vacated by a newly married couple. The groom had taken a new job in Malaya and left his bride with neighbors. She would live for a few months at Kyambogo in a house with friends on the school compound, until he settled in the new post and came back for her. He was due back any day now. Together, they would move to their new post.

In the headmaster's office, before I took possession of the house, I was greeted with an invitation to attend a sundowner at the home of one of the college's history masters. The headmaster ushered me into a nearby office and introduced me to my host, the young history professor named Brain Walton. Kathryn, Brian's wife, sat with him in the company of their house guest, Erin, a young woman of about twenty-three years. Dressed in a green blouse and pink culottes, Erin smiled beautifully. I noticed the yellow hair and freckles on her nose.

Brian said, "I say, the sundowner is soon. Come promptly at six o'clock, so you won't miss any of the antics."

Since I had not worked among the British in the tropics before and had no idea, I asked, "Sundowner, what's that?"

Brian and Kathryn, who had spent a honeymooning summer in Canada and America, exchanged smiling glances. Kathryn said, jokingly, "It's like an American cocktail party, held on the lawn at sundown, except it's more fun."

"Everyone comes," Brian added, "has drinks and toasts all around, while meeting everyone else."

I left them and walked up hill a short distance past school buildings and science labs, thinking of meeting my first students in just three days.

I found the two-bedroom house assigned to me empty. It had been recently cleaned, scrubbed from top to bottom. African servants moved my jumble of chemistry and biology books and bags in and made the beds, and all was ready for my occupancy. But as I walked through the house, my footsteps echoed softly. Although it was empty of former tenants, there lingered throughout the rooms, over most of the house, the smell of perfume. The house was empty except for the bed and bedding, and my unpacked trunks and suit-cases still rested in the hallway, awaiting my choice of a room for them.

I went through each room with the doors standing open, finding the rooms empty, mute, and receptive. The servant opened windows, bringing in wind that fretted and billowed the white curtains about. And yet, still lingered the odor of that perfume. It was a halting essence that spoke of a feminine presence. The scent was strongest in the large master bedroom. So I put my things in the small bedroom and got dressed in casual shorts and sports shirt, hoping I was appropriately dressed for the sundowner.

Inhabitants had apparently forgotten that *sundowner*, the word itself, referred to a single drink taken at the end of a hard day, usually a mixture of Malibu rum and pineapple juice and Angostura bitters. On the several tables set up on the manicured terraced lawn were numerous bottles of vodka, gin, bourbon, Irish whiskeys, Johnny Walker, Harvey's Bristol Cream, and various wines that had slipped through customs and made their way to the several tables. And now jibes of joy and "cheers" rang out as glasses clinked, then were raised over and over again among jokes and bright laughter, saluting everyone and everything.

A lot of liquor, beer, and wine, local and imported, flowed to and from glasses held in tanned hands and tipped to happily creased faces. Gaiety prevailed and goodwill rose in animated voices and wafted over the school compound. I was toasted several times by Elliot, the geography master, and again by Brian, and I was introduced to the occupants of the spacious lawn again by those who did not know we had met in the headmaster's office. After an hour—those sitting at tables now gladdened with the musical clink of empty bottles and glasses—the headmaster called for glasses to be filled for the sundowner. He made an impromptu announcement that there was an American on the staff and said, jokingly, that they should just remember that, in spite of our different views on education, America and England are still allies. Brendan, who was Irish, said something about the Irish Republic and if I met him in the staff room he'd teach me how to make a cup of real Irish tea. With that, someone corrected him: "Coffee, Brendan, Irish coffee." Allan, the staff Rugby coach, said he needed another bloke for the Rugby side and wondered whether I could join up. Responding to his vernacular, I said I was keen for it. The wives, led by Kathryn and Erin, were friendly and met me, a bachelor, with sparkling eyes.

Toward seven o'clock, the sun sparkled through trees. The headmaster saluted everyone, downed a stiff drink, said Cheer-io, and ambled off down the graveled road to his house. I was not clearheaded, having drunk a proffered glass of *waraga*, the local African drink—comparable to American gin or moonshine—and the shandies that Brendan had urged on me. By the time Elliot and his wife Susan raised their beer steins, making excuses to leave early for a trip to Kampala the next day, the party had thinned as couples drifted away, the sunlight fading, dusk replacing it. When I signaled the distracted, alcohol-bemused few still remaining that I too was leaving, it was to no one's notice. As I started uphill toward my house, out of the shadows of a mimosa tree stepped Erin. She stumbled against me as if she had drunk over her limit.

When I put up my hand to prevent her fall, I caught a whiff of the same perfume from my new house.

"I say, Moses, do you mind if I walk up to yours with you?"

"With me?" I was surprised.

"Yes, I left a few personal items in your house. This is a good time to retrieve them since Martin is coming back any day now."

"Are you...did you live here? Are you the couple who just left this house?"

"Martin and I jolly well loved it. I hope you won't mind terribly if I nip in and get my things." She was unsteady on her feet and almost missed the bottom step. My arm guided her up.

She wobbled directly to the master bedroom and, looking behind the door among noisy hangers, she soon held up her lacy night gowns and other garments, and the perfume odor engulfed us. It struck me then why her things had not been seen by the servants or me. The doors were all the way open, and no one looked behind them.

But still holding her night clothes, Erin swayed, suddenly seemed weak, and sank tumbling to the floor among her personal items.

"Erin! Erin!" I called her several times, then knelt beside her, got my arms under her and lifted her to the bed. I looked out of the window down to the sundowner, thinking, *What do I do now? Should I go for one of the women to help? Should I go down there for help?*

But all the lights were out and it was dark. I didn't want to leave her alone that time of night. Besides, what Erin needed right then was to sleep. I shook Erin a couple of times, but she was snoring. *Better to let her sleep in the bed that she was used to sharing with Martin.* I covered her with a sheet, put a pillow under her head and then went to my room, where I unpacked and went to bed.

The next morning, I was awakened by the crunch of gravel under Landover tires and the blaring of a horn. I open the door, then quickly Brian was in the living room with another red-faced chap whose eyes were angry and his mouth couldn't stay still.

Brian said, "I say, Moses, we have searched the whole blasted compound. Have you seen Erin? She didn't sleep at ours last night, and here is Martin just returned, looking for her."

Before I answered them, my eyes glanced toward the master bedroom, and Brian and Martin rushed in there and found Erin still asleep, with her lacy night gowns, still on hangers, lying on the bed beside her. Martin took Erin into his arms. She was fully dressed in the clothes she'd worn the previous evening. His frowns changed to satisfied smiles when he saw my wrinkled bed and me still in night clothes.

He took his bride away, over his shoulder. She was finally awake, and embarrassed and apologetic. "Gee, Moses, after all the trouble I caused, I suppose you'll never speak to me again."

Martin's face relaxed, and I could see Erin and I had provided an amusing story that would be told over and over at future sundowners.

MONKEY MISTAKE

It was like a miniature game park in Entebbe near the banks of Lake Victoria. I don't know what it is like now, but in 1965, you entered it by going downhill on the highway to the town, but instead of going through the town and left to past the capitol buildings and on to the airport, you veered left around the edge of the lake where the road was edged with many trees. And if you followed it, you turned into a road where close-set trees guarded it and vegetation rose up on high banks.

Here the trees that set back from the winding road were very high and festooned with vines, some long and heavy, looping down connecting trees some slim and lanky.

Birds dove in here—gulls, weavers. Several crested cranes sailed among the vegetation. And high, high above it all, with swinging vibrant, playful sounds, were the monkeys. They gallivanted up and down the tops of the high trees and branches swinging like circus acrobats swinging by each other on limbs branches and vines. When one came near another, he flicked out an arm or a leg or even its tail and then swung by its arm to another limb or vine. It was as if they were trained circus performers. Watching them was so entertaining. That was a place I liked to visit whenever I went to Entebbe airport and had waiting time. I wanted to see the birds and the performing monkeys in that park.

Actually, it was not an organized park, but just a natural place for animals to be. Off limits to hunters. No one disturbed, hunted, or molested them in any way.

This time that I am referring to was on a Sunday morning. I am sure I had taken someone that morning to catch an early flight and thought I'd drive through the park for a chance to watch the birds and monkeys. I parked down under these tall trees. I am a biologist and should know the names of those trees, but now I am not sure of the names. I only know they were quite tall, sixty or seventy feet up, with many high branches and vines clinging from tree to tree.

I'd been parked only a few minutes when the monkeys began their swinging and scampering up and over from tree to tree and from limb to vine, up and down and over, doing flips and making soft sounds as they flipped by hands over each other. They behaved as if they knew they had an audience to please. I marveled at their timing and agility. They touched each other, catching and swinging by and flipping as they made momentarily contact.

Then, as I watched in disbelief, one missed a connection and was falling below a tree limb, a place devoid of vines. When this monkey plummeted toward the earth, I became alarmed. I thought there'd be a monkey below to catch him, to break his fall. Or a tree limb or vine would be under it to stop its fall, but he quickly fell on and on from a high distance, with a thudding crash into the bush, striking the earth near my car.

I stood there, thinking the monkey would jump up and run to a tree, swing up, and join the group. But as I hovered over it, there was no sign of life I could detect. No chest rising and falling. No sign of life. I stood for about five minutes. Then I opened the car's trunk, thinking to put the monkey in the trunk. It did not move. I thought the fall had killed it. I would take it to the lab in Kyambogo and ask the principal for directions about how to handle it, what I should do with it.

But by the time I was ready to load the monkey into my car, it leaped up and ran through bushes, back to a tree, ran up it and was soon swinging as before. I thought, yes, a monkey made a mistake, but it has already corrected it.

I watched to see if there was any change in the behavior of the monkeys. If there were any, I couldn't tell. They were back performing as they did when I first arrived.

Have We Forgotten

The Teachers for East Africa Experience of the 1960s were all Americans, but we are each quite different. We came from different parts of America. We came with our own unique stories, backgrounds, and mythologies. We came with our prejudices but packed them away, hid them. But they were always with us.

I came from Mississippi. When I left there in 1961, they were using dogs to herd young school children into cattle pens in the fairgrounds in Jackson, Mississippi, because these black school children were marching down to the bus station to see the Freedom Riders and the sit-ins instead of going to school in segregated classrooms.

Back then we heard about the "culture shock" of going into a new country where the rules are different. You no longer feel restricted by the social rules that govern you at home, but you don't yet feel responsible for the rules of your host country.

I witnessed a young housewife from America openly experiencing a bit of culture shock in the Airline Curio Shoppe at the airport in Kano, Nigeria. I was in back of her as she stood by her husband with a little blonde child on her hip. She watched the black stewardesses and pilots as they walked out to board their planes along with most of the passengers, who were also black. She gently elbowed her husband in his side and said, "Honey!" He answered, "Yeah?" and she said in a slightly bewildered voice, "Everyone here is black!" He looked at her and smiled and said, "Well, dear, it *is* Africa..."

In describing our coming to Africa, we had to deal with culture shock. What did we do? What mores did we respect? We had to answer questions of whom do we love? How much do we drink? How late do we stay out on school nights? How do we treat the local people? What determined our moral compass? We were free to choose!

We had the British as a standard for teaching and treating "native" servants. We had to decide: Do we follow their lead, or do we slowly change what they have in place? What we did then says something about our character. Yet no one knows of our choices and actions but us. Do we question? Do we reflect? Do we teach more to memorize or do we mix it with problem solving? Do we remember always that we are teachers? Even when we are not in the classrooms, whenever we act, we teach.

What do we see? Do we notice that the upper level economy is not in the hands of Africans? Do we notice that most of the students we teach have parents who are mostly house servants, drivers, or yard-care workers or small-unit farmers? What do we think of that? Are we invited to the Europeans-only clubs? What do we do when we are asked to join?

I am just asking, not accusing. We are all Americans and we are all in this together. We were passionate about teaching in Africa and we still are.

The reason for interest in our writing is because the independence of the three East African countries remains associated with the years of our coming to teach. We Americans came to teach at their celebration of freedom, which came almost two hundred years after we attained our own independence from the same country that held them in bondage.

We taught the students who saw their countries gain their independence. We taught the students who became the first free leaders and government officials, the first free teachers who grew up in a free Uganda, a free Kenya, and a free Tanzania.

To read more writings from other participants, see *Teaaki Wiki: Stories and Lessons Learned from the Teachers for East Africa Experience of the 1960*: http://bit.ly/2emMdzL

PREVIEW: NZINGA
AFRICAN WARRIOR QUEEN

Across the savannah and into the green mountains, people shouted her name:

"Nzinga, Nzinga, Child of the Flame!"
"Nzinga, Daughter of the Old Ngola, Savior of Ndongo!"

In the governor's palace Luanda, the Portuguese courtiers whisper in shock: *A woman!*

Sent to make a treaty with the invaders, Nzinga of Angola is swept into world history, a generation after Elizabeth I ruled England. For forty years, Queen Nzinga fights to destroy the imperial colonists who seek to enslave her people.

This fictional biography delivers exhilarating adventure and passionate stories of friendship, love, and family. Luminous storytelling brings to life the Angolan culture in a flourishing African kingdom, now lost, where early maps of West Africa call out: *"Here reigned the celebrated Queen Nzinga!"*

Read an early chapter from the historical fiction novel, *Nzinga, African Warrior Queen.*

1.

CELEBRATION

THE OLD KING OF NDONGO, the Ngola Kilijua, returned home in the dry season, riding in a litter. The African savannah shimmered in the August sun. The mat of amber grasses swayed and sighed like gentle waves on a calm sea. On its surface the grass rippled and undulated, but deep down in the gray earth the thirsty roots of the long blades gripped like tenuous fingers, grasping and squeezing the hard soil, desperately seeking water. For months, night and day, the roots sent upward the flow that greened the savannah. But now the skin of the earth did not respond. Relief could come only from the clouds. Yet above the swaying grasses, the sky's gaze remained serenely blue, a solitary white plume of cloud playing across its face.

A fierce wave ran through the swaying grass mat, causing a steady forward motion accompanied by sounds unfamiliar to ears that cherished the music of the grasses, to those inhabitants who sang in the grasses, ate in the grasses, gave birth, lived, and died in the grasses. For them a different music played. These beings moving through the grass so briskly brought bold music, challenging and violent. Sounds drifted over the savannah, of human voices and human feet, of knives.

Ubolo, Upolo!

Plonk, plik, ple, plomp!

Whoosh, whee, clee, clompik!

Spisffff, nopffff, wheeeee zzip!

Spears remained at the ready, but were not needed for the work that feet and arms did.

Yet the grasses didn't yield at once to the sound or movement of invading feet. The strong, thick stalks fought to survive on the African veldt and refused to bow under the onrush of the first cruel steps.

Only after constant battering did the grass give up its springing counter-attack, after thousands of feet marched it into submission.

This charging wave advanced swiftly, orderly, rhythmically across the vastness of the veldt, like the wind filling a void with its methodical, cyclic sweep. Warthog, dik-dik, sable wildebeest, gazelle, rhino, and lion sniffed the air, puzzled. Then the scent told all. They quickly detoured. Some sprang away in the face of this hungry, surging throng, filling the air above the grasses with their leaping escape. Others disturbed the stalks with crawling, rushing, and digging retreats from this mass that needed to feed itself as it moved. Small groups scouted out from the sides at intervals, but then, after a squeal from prey, withdrew back to the main body as if driven back by the rhythm of drums.

The voices of the callers never ceased. Chants varied, but the rhythms maintained, as though the mass traveled on cadence. And it did, unless some obstacle moved into its path; then the tempo slowed or sped to a shrill cry.

"Mbacka! Mbacka!"

"Cambambe, Uuuhu, Uuuhu Uuuhuuaa!"

This chant issued from the throat of deep-chested men with lean brown bodies that remained dry of sweat from sunrise to early afternoon under the equatorial sun. Drums hidden in the moving ranks underscored and confirmed the chant.

"Mbacka, Mbacka, Cambambe, Uuuhuu!"

This wave of marching warriors was ordered, disciplined, and armed with spears, knives, bows and arrows, and a few captured guns. The army was massive in depth and sweep. A soldier at the front ordered to walk back along its ranks would take at least a day to reach the end of the column. In addition to the trained soldiers, the army's numbers were swollen by captives and displaced refugees fleeing the Portuguese, forming a body that reached back toward Luanda. Others who came along were the curious people from Ndongo who joined the army as it passed through their villages.

From far back in the flowing throng, yet moving to the same rhythm, a clutch of muscular warriors pressed forward, supporting litters bearing their leader and his ministers. As the slightly bent bodies and running bearers tired, they shifted the poles to other warriors who stepped in to relieve them. From the side of one litter, a messenger was dispatched to the drummers, who at once changed the tempo. The whole army sped up its march as though readied for a great emergency. The chant raced along.

"Mbacka, Mbacka. Cambambe, Huh, Huh!"

For months, since the Ngola had left to fight a battle, runners returned daily to Mbacka, the royal village, racing with all their strength to carry news to their leader's people, to tell how the Ngola rested, how he slept, how he fought, how he won and how he lost, and why. Now the runners didn't have so far to go when they left the army to run to the Mbanza, the Ngola's palace:

"The Ngola is coming!"

"The Ngola is near!"

Finally they had only a short distance to run. Panting to catch their breath, for they ran at top speed all the way, they had only one message.

"The Ngola is here!"

The change in the movement of the army was caused by its surroundings. The grass underfoot collapsed now into a soft cushion. In the distance loomed green bushes, then trees, and finally a forest. Cool air struck them in the face. The sound that had been a murmur at midday now roared in their ears. Cutting through the chants, it had more power than the book of the drums. The marchers gave themselves up to that roar, moving almost as if in a dance. It didn't matter that their pulses pounded in their temples and they were near collapse. An inner sense of release drove them toward the Cambambe waterfalls, where the Ngola's palace, the Mbanza, stood on a hill above the Cuanza River.

The column split into equal halves as it came through the forest into the clearing, fanning out along the banks of the river some distance away from the Mbanza. People poured out of the villages and ancestral shrines along the way as the warriors, now leaping and dancing, paraded in front of them. The praise singers heralded the arrival of the Ngola, dropping to their knees to honor him.

Along the banks, and even back in the forest, the builders had already set to work with permission from spiritual leaders and the prime minister, cutting down trees to construct the Ngola's round houses. Even while the rear units were still moving, the Ngola's fire-brand was brought forward and the cooks set up to prepare food.

The royal drummers with the Ngola's ceremonial instruments took over in a gigantic festival of drumming that echoed up and down the river and through the whole of Ndongo. The dancers came, women first, undulating and calling, laughing playfully, chanting and leaping in a contest, one unit striving to outdo the other. The strident, haunting sounds from the bushbuck horns broke all inhibitions, calling everyone to come and chant.

"Ngola! Ngola! Ngola! Rainmaker!"

When the eyes seeking the king could endure the waiting no longer, a wild frenzy of drumming brought him through the crowd. The army opened its ranks to a spear-bearing phalanx of warriors who bolted wildly through the crowd like lightning, cutting down a score of onlookers who blocked the way. These were left lying to the side, dying in their own blood, while litter bearers bore the Ngola forward with dazzling speed and hoisted him high above the cheering crowd. People fell prostrate on the ground, averting their eyes from his brilliance and clasping their hands above their heads.

〰

While the people in the palace enclosure celebrated the return of the Ngola, the returning soldiers celebrated outside, a safeguard against the army bringing back pestilence. None of the people who came with the Ngola could enter the palace for ten days. They scrubbed in the river several times and waited. The formal celebration for their return had to come later.

In the meantime, the celebration inside the palace lasted long into the night and continued for several nights. The moon was high and bright. They told stories and reenacted battles, embraced their age mates, created the music of battles, and danced. A feast began afresh each day, with plantain beer, millet beer, and palm wines.

The merrymaking at the palace was mixed with cries throughout the kingdom of people who were related to Chief Kassa, who had betrayed the Ngola's plans to the Portuguese. Although the Ngola had granted Kassa a chiefdom that lay between Luanda and Massangano, Kassa had family and property in different parts of Ndongo. As soon as the Ngola arrived home, he held a meeting with his chiefs to give orders about the renegade Chief Kassa.

"Burn his land. Take his people and make them servants in other families. Take his cattle. Anyone who is hungry may kill and cook his goats. They may dig his yams, harvest his cassava, and winnow his grain. Let people take whatever is his tonight throughout the kingdom. Do it quickly. Let none of them flee. Leave his land bare for another chief and his people."

As soon as the order was given, people began disappearing from the celebration, heading for parts of Ndongo where Kassa was known to have property. They wanted to be present at the moment when the Ngola's soldiers arrived. Once the Ngola issued such an order, all possessions of the offender could be claimed by any loyal citizen of Ndongo. They knew Kassa's villagers had heard the news and were busy hiding all they owned. This effort would surely fail once the king withdrew his protection. So people watched and waited for the soldiers to arrive, and when their work was done, the people pounced on what was left. After that, fires blazed in the night in parts of the kingdom, and some heard Kassa's people crying for their lost possessions and lost honor.

What the Ngola ordered was the least costly price paid for disloyalty to the Ngola. The greatest price was death to the disloyal one and possibly his family. Many of the soldiers who fought alongside the Ngola were rewarded with Kassa's cows, his land, his servants, and any goods found in his houses. Kassa's punishment didn't end with this night. His army would be watched night and day. After the Portuguese army left them, Kassa's army would be under periodic siege from the Ngola's chiefs, his fields near Luanda would be burned, and his houses raided. Anyone who injured Kassa's property in any way received the protection of the Ngola.

〔〕

The Ngola made preparations to send parts of his army and his chiefs to their various homes across Ndongo. He visited nearby shrines to pay homage to the gods and ancestors, and he presided at rain-making ceremonies. Ten days after his return, the Ngola and his two wives sat in their private common room inside the palace at Mbacka. The royal children were brought in.

Kaningwa, the first wife, was slender with small breasts, and was known throughout Ndongo as a great beauty. She wore stylish African clothes made from many-colored kente cloth and the best fashions and cloth from the Portuguese trade. She was a favorite among many wives of the Ngola's chiefs, who copied the styles Kaningwa wore and talked of her constantly. She invited them to visit in the palace and spoke freely with them of her family and the Ngola's business.

Kaningwa took the lead in welcoming the Ngola. She ordered servants to bring drinks and then was the first to drink and fall down in front of the Ngola. Now she sat nearby, first looking at him with limpid eyes, then moving her slender neck to show the Ngola her profile and her hair piled high, the way she'd been told hair was worn in Lisbon. She ignored her two daughters, who sat on pillows on the floor. Her son Mbande, who was eight rains old, sat beside her. With two rainy seasons each year, the Portuguese would call him four years old. At Kaningwa's signal, the boy knelt in front of his father, who lifted him up and brought him near.

The Ngola smiled. "Mbande, boy, you have come along. The rains are making you grow as well as the cassava." Mbande smiled shyly. His father said, "You are a prince, my son. You needn't be shy or look away from anyone. You must look straight at them and learn what they are thinking."

Mbande later told his mother that he wasn't shy; he simply wasn't interested in what was being discussed. Mbande was never able to concentrate on anything except those things of interest to himself. Nothing held his attention for long.

"My mind runs on other things."

He'd love to ask his father about the big fish he'd seen the fishermen take away from the river, and why it flipped and flashed its silver sides in an effort to escape, and how it caused the men to bleed by puncturing them with its blade-like fins. He also wanted to ask his father about the feeling you get when you swim and feel the buoyancy of water against your body. He knew, however, these weren't the things that interested his father.

Even as his father spoke after returning from the war, Mbande at eight seasons old was thinking of the stool his father sat on, with its beautiful animal skins and how the smooth fur felt against his skin. He liked to see other boys wrestle and sweat. He could wrestle, and several times he'd shown his father that he did it well, but he didn't like to fall and roll in the dirt.

His father was talking, asking one of the court servants to bring something into the room. Mbande hadn't been paying attention but now he heard, " . . . present for Mbande."

"You're going to like this, my son," the Ngola said. A servant brought in a rolled bark-cloth tied into a bundle. At the king's signal, the servant unfurled it on the floor with a flourish.

Several wives and women servants gasped. Mbande cringed, clinging to his father, who laughed.

The king said, "Your mothers may be afraid, but surely the Ngola's son isn't afraid of a crocodile's skin. This is for you. You will have a belt, knife holder, and arrow holder made from it. Just like the ones I have."

"Thank you, sir," Mbande said. He clasped his hands in front of the Ngola.

The Ngola's daughters approached, and he hugged them and allowed them to sit on his knee. The king remarked how they had grown. They told what they'd learned while he was away and showed the baskets they'd woven. The oldest one showed him a beaded gourd. They talked about the animals they'd seen.

"A herd of gazelles dashed by the palace gate. There are still giraffes near here, feeding in the trees. Lions roared late one night, shaking us from our beds."

Kaningwa's servant brought in a drum of solid, shiny brown wood, shaped like an antelope. The children could strike it, but no one seemed to know how to play it. The Ngola gave each child a packet that contained colored beads from Portugal plus the strong bristles from an elephant and a warthog. The girls smiled with pleasure. Their mother and a chorus of servants assured the Ngola that it was the nicest possible present and that the girls would make wonderful things from it.

〇

Batayo, the Ngola's younger wife, was tall, timid, and well-shaped. She dressed only in African clothes and wore her hair in a handsome basket-weave, the style of which she changed often. She spoke softly and openly, saying exactly what she thought, but quickly apologizing if she offended.

Batayo waited patiently for the Ngola to turn to her that evening. She truly loved all the royal children and shared in their joy. Many times she told her friend Sufalu, the king's seer, that she wished in her heart for a boy to make the Ngola happy. She'd followed all advice given her. She wished her mother had been there to oversee the birth of the boy she'd lost. Yet she didn't envy Mbande his position as the only male child.

A servant brought in Batayo's new baby daughter, who had just awakened. Newly washed and oiled, the child was a bit thin.

"And who is this one?" asked the Ngola.

"No one until you give it a name," Batayo said. Because the Ngola had been away for more than a year, the child had been given a temporary name that only became official if and when the Ngola sanctioned it.

"What do you wish it to be named?" asked the Ngola.

"She's been called Nzinga."

"A good name."

"I am so sorry, my Ngola, it isn't a boy."

"Are you sure?" asked the king, who already knew, but he turned the naked body of the child to see its sex. "Yes, it is a girl. But what does that matter? She'll be like her mother." He held the child on his knee. She grasped his hand and looked straight at him. "What is this? She seems to understand everything I'm saying."

The Ngola kept talking to the child, telling her where he'd been and how at Luanda he'd seen a whale. He murmured to Nzinga that some people didn't know how to treat her father, like a certain chief who'd betrayed him in battle. But she'd help to show them how to treat her father when she grew up. The child smiled and tried to raise his big hand with hers.

"Did you see that?" said the Ngola. He and Batayo looked at each other and smiled in remembrance of their past joy. "This child is special."

A wild jealousy grew inside Kaningwa, though she had been elated by the attention given her son. She fawned over Mbande and looked sweetly at her husband, keeping his attention as long as possible.

"Listen, husband. Mbande can tell the names of all his fore-fathers, from the First Ngola, Blacksmith Prince. Go ahead, Mbande, recite them for your father."

Mbande recited them quickly and expertly. His mother nodded approvingly when he was done. Then she passed slowly in front of the king, arching her long beautiful neck, and moistening her lips with a flick of the tongue.

The children, other wife, and servants were dismissed when he retired with Kaningwa to the inner quarters with the iron rings on the door.

⬜⬜⬜

The next day, Kaningwa gossiped that Batayo disappointed the Ngola twice, not yet having given birth to a male child. "The first time she lost her baby and now, the second time," Kaningwa said to Chief Oyimbu's wife, "even though she pestered the royal cook for tender vegetables and the choicest cuts of meat. Even though she rested and thought good thoughts, she only managed to give birth to a little skinny baby girl. Now Batayo too is skinny."

Kaningwa also said to the chief's wife, "And, my cousin and friend, did you see? The Ngola barely glanced at her all evening."

She planted a servant in Batayo's quarters to watch and report. Whenever Kaningwa got the chance, she stole a sidelong look at Batayo. "Wretched woman," she said to friends, but she wasn't sorry for Batayo, who had been the favorite, nearly taking over because she danced so well and played many musical instruments. Batayo was wrong if she thought she'd always get attention.

Kaningwa told Chief Kadu's wife, "After what happened yesterday, I'm sure Mbande will be the Ngola when the Ngola dies . . . I mean, someday. Then let them all watch out. It will be far different." For one, by Ndongo custom, when the new Ngola was anointed, all other male children would be killed. Batayo should consider herself lucky she didn't have a son, who would only die when Mbande became Ngola. Kaningwa remained determined to tie her son close to her by any means possible. *"I must teach Mbande to be cunning. If only he was a little less playful."*

Kaningwa gazed proudly at her children, who were playing with their gifts from the king. She looked at the chief's young wife again. "Why did Batayo call this last baby Nzinga? The nerve of her. It is a girl, and yet Batayo gives it part of the name of an ancient king. Well, we shall see."

■ ■ ■

To read more, find Nzinga, African Warrior Queen
from your bookseller:
Print ISBN: 978-1-939423-40-5
Ebook ASIN: B01HLTGGRS
http://bit.ly/2dROnv0

PREVIEW: THE SKY HIGH ROAD

A footballer faces crushing odds—against the Lord's Liberation Army!
How to keep hope kindled for a brighter future?

Jason, a 17-year-old soccer player in a Ugandan village, is worried about his O-levels and grieving his father's death from AIDS. His grandmother sends Jason and his sister Katura on a journey to her home village. That unwanted chore turns to catastrophe when they are enslaved as child-soldiers in the Lord's Liberation Army.

Jason and Katura battle their insane captors, who inflict hideous harm on the children they kidnap. Escaping, Jason and Katura encounter both helpers and new dangers on the journey home. Can they bring home more than a solar lantern for their grandmother, carrying new light for their future in Uganda?

Read an early chapter from the young-adult novel, *The Sky High Road*.

◆

Jason's father is dead and his mother lay dying of AIDS in the back room. His grandmother had come all the way from her home at Nanansi to take care of Mama. Now she was scheming to send him and his sister Katura away.

Jason would never say "No" to Grandma. He'd never say to her that he wouldn't do something she asked. That would be disrespectful. He didn't say he wouldn't go. He didn't say anything. He kept quiet and went outside to tend the goats and check the fence.

His family was a zoo observed by the park animals, or so it seemed. The animals watched Jason's family through the ten-foot-tall metal fence with two strands of barbed wire running along its top next to the big game park. Hartebeest, aggressive warthogs, huge elephants, and colorful zebras were all familiar visitors to the silver fence managed by his father.

Jason's father was a decorated park ranger. With one shot he felled a buffalo that charged a Land Rover full of tourists, mostly women and children. He had captured members of a band of poachers who raided the Uganda Queen Elizabeth National Park and hunted white rhinos almost to extinction, killing them for their horns.

Before the fence, the animals had wandered over the family property; sleek brown antelopes ate his mother's garden vegetables; elephants left piles of steaming dung on the path in front of their house and trampled the lawn. Goats got lost to leopards while Jason attended school.

He knew it was dangerous to go into the game park. Although when his father was alive he had warned Jason, when Father was away Jason had climbed over the fence to get a soccer ball kicked there, and he'd hiked in the park if the animal herds drifted away. Confident he could always climb back over speedily without the animals seeing him, he'd often visited the park. He'd practiced moving in and out like his father.

Now was a good time to do it again, to escape Grandma's demands. No buffalo or warthog or rhino was visible. None of the big cats like lions, or cheetahs lived here. He could outrun any other animal. Wearing tennis shoes, he would be fast like one time when his father had caught him. Daddy swatted him with a tree branch. *"Jason, you better listen. Animals can smell you before you can see them."*

Jason had smooth brown skin and short curly hair. He was listed on his soccer roster at Budo School as five feet eleven inches tall. He was muscular with strong arms and legs. He leaped up, caught the top strand of the fence, muscled up, and twisting, flipped his body over, and landed on springing feet in the park. Over the fence, twenty yards ahead, he scanned down the hill to the tourist station, the lake, and the parking lot. No animals around, so he went to the edge of the flat park and looked through the low trees and tall grasses. A group of tourists were walking with a ranger toward the lake. Others stood on the verandah, gazing after them. Everything looked normal in the park. Suddenly, he became aware of movement behind him. When he whirled around there were two giraffes nibbling on high tree branches. Oops! They weren't there the last time he looked. Instinctively, shivers ran up the back of his neck. How could he have been so mistaken?

He turned abruptly and headed back. Several monkeys in the distance cavorted in the bush and low trees between him and the fence, and a little farther down, a water buffalo coming up the hill. He wanted to run, but he knew better. He grabbed the highest barbed-wire strand, muscled up, and flipped himself into the yard. Relieved and ashamed, he heard Daddy's warning again in his head. *"Jason, animals can smell you before you see them."*

Then he went around to the front of the house to watch the park rangers—dressed in their green uniforms and yellow hard hats like Daddy used to wear—unload long bare eucalyptus logs to put up the long-awaited electricity light posts near the baobab trees.

He'd come outside just to get away from Grandma's talk. After checking the fence and the goats and wandering dangerously into the park, he crept back inside the spacious living room.

Grandma was straining, looking over her eyeglasses to see the labels on the new medicine bottles that the AIDS nurses brought for Mama. The nurses visited with medicine and advice at least once a week. Grandma grumbled that she could hardly see in the bright daylight, and her difficulties at night were worse. Her choices for lighting were a smoky lantern, a torch, or candles. She straightened up and looked at him intently. "Please, go to my house and bring back the solar lamp."

When Grandma gained that lamp, she had lost her son. Daddy had bought this special lamp for her when he went to a conference for rangers in Nairobi. She bragged that this lamp needed no oil. You set it out in the bright sun and its strips soaked up light and stored it. At night it just glowed. It was a solar lamp.

"If we bring your lamp here, what will you use when you go back home?" He said that just to delay her. He was just reaching for any excuse he could get.

Katura, his fourteen-year-old sister, was in the bedroom off the hallway making beds. Grandma rarely allowed the children into the back room where their dangerously ill mother rested. Although the visiting nurses said that AIDS could only be spread by sexual intercourse and the blood and other liquids from sick patients, she was very cautious.

Jason couldn't say how he felt to see Mama lying there; sometimes she barely breathed. She had lost a lot of weight and never called out or laughed or even told him and Katura to do chores or homework. His heart thumped; he lowered his head and looked away every time he glimpsed her. Daddy was already dead of it, and now Mama might go the same way.

Jason knew Grandma wasn't mad at him; she wanted to convince him. That was her way. He knew she loved both him and Katura. They visited her at Nanansi last year, and it was the happiest time they had ever had. Even though he loved Grandpa and especially his jokes and the funny things he did with them, Jason wasn't aiming on leaving his grandmother all alone here to take care of Mama and Asia, their baby sister. What if Mama died or something while he was gone? It would be like he'd abandoned her.

Grandma wasn't angry when she looked straight at him, but he knew right away it wasn't the long-suffering "ask me anything" grandmother that they were used to. Although she had the sweetest smiles and looks most of the time, she didn't have them this time. She was all serious, like she had been thinking all the time. She had been up nights for the two weeks she'd been here to take care of Mama.

"What do you mean, Jason? What will I use when I go back? We'll cross that puddle when it rains. And it's not even rainy season. Do you think I have only one lamp at home? I have the old one and a beautiful one that your grandpa bought for me years ago on a trip to Kampala, long before Katura there was born." She pointed to his baby sister with the hand that held the plastic medicine containers. "Asia wasn't even thought of back then." She paused. "But the very best one is the solar lamp."

"Daddy bought us a lamp, too, and lots of nice things from a *duka* in Mbarara." Katura said wistfully from the bedroom door.

"Your daddy did a lot of things . . . good things. He did . . . bad things, too. He didn't take care of himself or his family." She averted her half-closed eyes and twisted her mouth firmly to one side as if she was avoiding taking an unpleasant medicine. She looked more intently at the medicine bottles. Jason knew by her looks and pauses this was unpleasant for her; yet, it was something she had to talk about. "AIDS kills people . . . more people die from hiding the truth. They cannot or will not see." She repeated this every day.

By her action he could tell it was a painful subject; her sweet familiar face soured with frowns and grimaces, and her eyes looked at you and through you. She must be thinking about her only son now dead and her responsibility to take care of his wife and children. She reminded them again that by his careless actions their father had killed himself.

Katura and Jason heard from the nurses who brought the medicine about prevention and the danger of contracting AIDS. Now that Grandma had started in on the topic, the whole painful thing was coming out again, because she insisted on going over everything to keep their minds focused on their safety.

Her words hurt Jason. "I would love to see Grandpa, but can't I wait and go there with you?"

"I won't be leaving here for some time. I can't leave your mother. I have lost my son. I won't go through that again. Don't you remember your father? Is he already dead and gone in your minds?" Over the tops of the medicine bottles, she stared at them. "Katura, don't you remember him? . . . How he loved you and took you everywhere in the park? You rode up on his shoulders, frolicking and seeing everything below you. Don't you both remember his wide, prideful grin, his green uniform and yellow park ranger hat? What about his courage when he ran the poachers out of the park? They returned and stole everything while the family was away. They even stole lamps and tablecloths off of the table."

Then she paused and turned away, folding her apron and wiping away tears. "Your father was about to get electricity here, but the main lines were so far away. It is taking longer than anyone thought. But now I need a good lamp to read medicine bottles to save your mother's life."

"I could go to the stores and get a small lamp with a wick, and we could just wait awhile. You shouldn't be here alone, just you and Katura."

"You and Katura will go to Grandpa to get my solar lamp while I stay and look after your mother and the baby," Grandmother said in a firm voice.

He looked at his grandmother then as if she had gone crazy. When Katura heard her name, she came out of the bedroom and stared, too. "No, Grandma! That can't happen," she blurted out.

Her words made Katura and Jason rebel. "No, Grandma! It is not nearly right. I know you want what is best, but I am kind of the man here."

"Yes," she said quickly, "but if your father is an example, we have seen what a man who does not know can do as a leader. That's why I want both you and Katura to learn to see the dangers and to gain the knowledge to fight them."

"Now, Grandma, you can't do everything by yourself. You're trying to do it. But it won't work."

Katura spoke up. "Grandma, do you know what you are saying? We just couldn't leave you alone *no how*."

They stood firmly against her. This time they would disobey.

■ ■ ■

To read more, find *The Sky High Road*
from your bookseller:
Print ISBN: 978-1-939423-30-6
Ebook ASIN: B00Y6104EG/
http://bit.ly/2dZ8aDG

ABOUT THE AUTHOR

Moses Leon Howard is an American writer and educator. He has written for children and adults for fifty years.

A retired community college dean, biology teacher, assistant high school principal, and counselor/mentor for students at risk, Mr. Howard now lives in Washington State.

In addition to his career as an educator in the U.S., Mr. Howard served as a Fulbright Fellow in Africa and spent ten years training medical technologists and preparing secondary school teachers in Kampala, Uganda.

Also by Moses L. Howard:
Nzinga, the Africa Queen
The Sky High Road
The Human Mandolin
The Ostrich Chase

Writing as Musa Nagenda:
Dogs of Fear: A Story of Modern Africa
The Ostrich Egg Shell Canteen

Learn more and find more publications by Mr. Howard, at
http://jugumpress.com/MosesHoward/

Follow Mr. Howard on Facebook at
https://www.facebook.com/MosesLHoward/

Read previews of fiction by Moses Howard in the following pages.

About Jugum Press

Jugum Press, a small independent publisher, presents an eclectic collection of fiction, historic monographs, memoirs, and the *Opera en Español* series.

Nzinga, African Warrior Queen
by Moses L. Howard

> Nzinga, in history and legend, is a brilliant leader during a time of violent upheaval. This fictional biography brings to life the Angolan culture in a flourishing 17th century African kingdom, where early explorers' maps of West Africa call out: "Here reigned the celebrated Queen Nzinga!"

A Boy from Wannaska
by Marjorie W. Mortensen

> Sparkling tales of life in a tiny northern Minnesota town amidst first-generation Scandinavian immigrants in the early twentieth century.

Journey Into Gold Country: Memories of a Forty-Niner
by Ralph Buckingham; foreword by Charles Barker

> Three wild years in the California Gold Rush, remembered in tranquility sixty years later by a New England younger son of a youngest son who went to seek his fortune.

Jugum Press titles are available at online stores, and you can request these books from your local bookseller.

Find print and ebook editions
and sign up to receive notice of new books
by Moses L. Howard and other writers at:
www.jugumpress.com

www.ingramcontent.com/pod-product-compliance
Lightning Source LLC
Chambersburg PA
CBHW071612040426
42452CB00008B/1320